INDUSTRIAL ENGINEERING

STRATEGIC PLANNING AND IMPLEMENTATION

DR. KUNWAR SANDIP

Made with ♥ on the Notion Press Platform
www.notionpress.com

To the visionaries who dreamed of a more efficient world,
To the problem-solvers who see potential in every challenge,
And to the unsung heroes in factories, offices, and supply chains
Who tirelessly pursue innovation and excellence.

This book is dedicated to you.

May it serve as a beacon of inspiration and a toolkit of knowledge
For those committed to shaping a future where systems are smarter,
Processes are greener, and the world works more harmoniously.

Contents

Foreword *vii*

Preface *ix*

Acknowledgements *xi*

Prologue *xiii*

1. Definition And Scope 1
2. History And Evolution 9
3. Systems Approach 15
4. Optimization And Efficiency 23
5. Time And Motion Study 27
6. Ergonomic Design And Human Factors 30
7. Forecasting And Demand Planning 32
8. Inventory Management 35
9. Production Scheduling 42
10. Total Quality Management (TQM) 47
11. Six Sigma And Lean Manufacturing 55
12. Linear Programming 60
13. Simulation And Modeling 71
14. Decision Analysis 82
15. Logistics And Distribution 92
16. Supply Chain Design And Optimization 104
17. Role Of IT And Automation 120
18. Data Analytics And Industrial Internet Of Things (IIoT) 132
19. Real-World Applications In Different Industries 145
20. Emerging Technologies 159
21. Sustainability And Green Manufacturing 169

Foreword

Industrial Engineering is more than a profession; it is the art and science of optimizing the world we live in. From enhancing production lines to revolutionizing supply chains, industrial engineers embody the quest for efficiency, sustainability, and innovation. This field stands as a beacon of progress, bridging human ingenuity and technological advancements to create smarter systems and processes.

In this book, we delve deep into the principles and applications of industrial engineering, exploring its transformative impact across industries. Through compelling case studies, cutting-edge research, and practical insights, the book offers readers a comprehensive understanding of how industrial engineering shapes the present and prepares us for the challenges of tomorrow.

Whether you're a student just beginning your journey in this fascinating field, a seasoned professional seeking fresh perspectives, or simply a curious mind intrigued by the mechanics of progress, this book is for you. It is a tribute to the thinkers and doers who continuously strive to improve the way we work and live.

As you turn the pages, may you be inspired by the dedication, creativity, and resilience that define industrial engineering. May it challenge you to reimagine possibilities and empower you to contribute to a better, more efficient world.

Preface

The ever-evolving world of **Industrial Engineering** stands at the forefront of innovation and progress. At its core, it is the discipline that transforms challenges into opportunities and inefficiencies into optimized solutions. Industrial engineering thrives on integrating people, technology, and processes to create systems that are not just productive but sustainable and adaptive to future needs.

This book emerges as a response to the growing demands of our rapidly changing industries and the evolving needs of society. It aims to provide a holistic understanding of the principles, practices, and methodologies of industrial engineering while equipping readers with the tools and insights needed to navigate this dynamic field.

Designed to cater to students, educators, practitioners, and enthusiasts alike, this book bridges theoretical foundations with practical applications. Through case studies, real-world examples, and thought-provoking discussions, it sheds light on the transformative power of industrial engineering in manufacturing, service industries, and beyond.

As you journey through its pages, my hope is that this book sparks curiosity, ignites passion, and fosters a commitment to continuous improvement. Industrial engineering is not merely a field of study or practice—it is a way of thinking,

Acknowledgements

This book is the culmination of numerous individuals' encouragement, guidance, and contributions. It stands as a testament to their unwavering support and belief in the significance of industrial engineering.

First and foremost, I extend my deepest gratitude to my mentors and the Expert from IT Industry Dr. Durgesh Singh, He is working in Tata Consultancy Services as Assistant Consultant, whose expertise and insights laid the foundation for much of the knowledge shared in these pages. Your encouragement fueled my dedication to this work.

To my colleagues and collaborators, your thought-provoking conversations and constructive feedback enriched the depth and breadth of this book. Thank you for challenging me to think beyond boundaries and for sharing your own experiences and perspectives.

To my family and friends, your patience and understanding as I immersed myself in this project were invaluable. Your faith in me provided the emotional strength to see this journey through to completion.

Finally, I owe a special thanks to all the professionals and pioneers in the field of industrial engineering whose work continues to inspire and pave the way for innovation. This book is but a small contribution to the incredible legacy you have built.

It is my sincere hope that this book empowers its readers to contribute meaningfully to the dynamic world of **Industrial Engineering.**

Prologue

The story of **Industrial Engineering** is intertwined with the evolution of human ingenuity. From the earliest days of crafting tools to the assembly lines of the industrial revolution, and now to the cutting-edge technologies shaping our modern world, industrial engineering has always been at the heart of progress.

This book is not just a guide to understanding industrial engineering; it is an exploration of how this field has shaped industries and societies. It is a tribute to the problem-solvers who stand at the intersection of innovation and efficiency, striving to create systems that are smarter, faster, and more sustainable.

As we face unprecedented challenges in a globalized, resource-constrained world, industrial engineering emerges as a beacon of hope—a discipline that not only seeks solutions but also builds a foundation for continuous improvement. This book invites you to journey through the principles, methods, and applications that drive this transformative field.

May this prologue serve as a doorway to the limitless possibilities of industrial engineering and inspire you to view the world through the lens of an engineer—where every system can be improved, and every challenge holds the seed of innovation.

CHAPTER ONE

DEFINITION AND SCOPE

Definition: Industrial Engineering is a branch of engineering that focuses on optimizing complex systems, processes, and organizations. It involves the application of engineering principles, mathematical methods, and scientific techniques to design, improve, and streamline operations in various industries. The goal is to increase efficiency, reduce waste, and enhance productivity while maintaining high standards of quality and safety. Industrial Engineering is a multidisciplinary field focused on optimizing complex systems, processes, and organizations to enhance efficiency, productivity, and quality. It combines principles from mathematics, science, engineering, and management to design and improve systems involving people, materials, equipment, energy, and information. Industrial engineers analyze workflows, reduce waste, and implement innovative solutions to streamline operations and maximize resource utilization. By focusing on both technical and human aspects, industrial engineering plays a crucial role in solving real-world challenges across industries such as manufacturing, healthcare, logistics, and service sectors, ultimately contributing to economic growth and operational excellence.

Scope: Industrial Engineering encompasses a wide range of activities aimed at optimizing complex systems, processes, and organizations. It includes work study and ergonomics to enhance workplace efficiency and comfort, production planning and control for effective resource allocation and scheduling, and quality management to ensure continuous improvement and high standards. Operations research involves applying mathematical models and optimization techniques, while supply chain management focuses on designing and managing logistics and distribution networks. Information systems utilize IT and automation to inform decision-making, and sustainability efforts aim to reduce environmental impact through green manufacturing. Industrial Engineers play a crucial role in various sectors, driving innovation and operational excellence.

The scope of Industrial Engineering is vast and encompasses a wide range of areas, including:

1. Work Study and Ergonomics: Work study and ergonomics are vital disciplines aimed at optimizing both productivity and worker well-being. Analyzing work processes involves observing and breaking down each task within a job to identify inefficiencies and eliminate unnecessary movements. By standardizing procedures and incorporating lean manufacturing principles, work study helps streamline operations, reduce waste, and improve overall efficiency. On the other hand, designing ergonomic workplaces focuses on creating environments that enhance worker comfort and productivity. This includes using adjustable furniture, proper lighting, and tools designed to fit the natural movements of the human body. Ergonomic principles ensure that workspaces are tailored to meet the diverse needs of workers, reducing the risk of strain and injury, and fostering a healthier, more engaged workforce. By integrating work study and ergonomics, organizations can achieve a harmonious balance between operational efficiency and employee satisfaction, leading to sustainable long-term success. Work study and ergonomics are critical aspects of industrial engineering focused on optimizing productivity and ensuring employee well-being. Work study involves analyzing and improving work methods, time management, and process efficiency to maximize output while minimizing resource waste. It includes techniques such as time studies, motion analysis, and workflow optimization to streamline operations. Ergonomics, on the other hand, emphasizes designing workspaces, tools, and processes to align with human capabilities and limitations, reducing physical strain and enhancing comfort. By integrating work study and ergonomics, industries can achieve higher efficiency, reduce workplace injuries, and promote employee satisfaction, ultimately contributing to a safer and more productive work environment.

- Analyzing work processes and improving work methods
- Designing ergonomic workplaces to enhance worker comfort and productivity

2. Production Planning and Control: Production planning and control are essential aspects of manufacturing that ensure efficient and effective operations. Forecasting demand and managing inventory involve predicting future customer demand using historical data, market trends, and statistical methods to ensure that the right quantity of products is available at the right time. Proper inventory management balances supply and demand, minimizing holding costs and preventing stockouts. On the other hand, scheduling production and optimizing resource allocation focus on creating a detailed plan for the manufacturing process. This includes determining the sequence of operations, assigning tasks to workstations, and allocating resources such as labor, machinery, and materials. By optimizing these elements, production planning ensures that manufacturing processes run smoothly, reduces downtime, and maximizes overall efficiency. Together, these practices help companies meet customer demands, reduce costs, and maintain a competitive edge in the market. Production planning and control (PPC) is a critical function in manufacturing that ensures the efficient utilization of resources to meet production goals. Production planning involves determining what to produce, how much to produce, and when to produce it, taking into account factors like demand forecasts, inventory levels, and resource availability. Production control, on the other hand, focuses on monitoring and regulating the production process to ensure it adheres to the planned schedule, quality standards, and cost constraints. Together, these processes streamline operations, minimize waste, and maintain a balance between supply and demand, ultimately enhancing productivity and customer satisfaction in manufacturing systems.

- Forecasting demand and managing inventory
- Scheduling production and optimizing resource allocation

3. Quality Management: Quality management is a comprehensive approach focused on ensuring that products and processes meet the highest standards of excellence. Implementing Total Quality Management (TQM) involves fostering a culture of quality across the entire organization, where every employee is committed to maintaining and enhancing quality in their respective roles. TQM emphasizes customer satisfaction, continuous improvement, and the involvement of all employees in quality initiatives. Six Sigma methodologies complement TQM by providing a structured, data-driven approach to identifying and eliminating defects in processes. Six

Sigma projects follow the DMAIC (Define, Measure, Analyze, Improve, Control) framework to achieve significant improvements in quality and efficiency. Ensuring product and process quality through continuous improvement involves regularly evaluating performance, identifying areas for enhancement, and implementing corrective actions. Techniques such as root cause analysis, process mapping, and statistical process control are used to monitor and improve quality continuously. By integrating TQM and Six Sigma, organizations can achieve higher levels of quality, reduce costs, and enhance customer satisfaction, ultimately leading to long-term success and competitiveness. Quality management is a comprehensive approach focused on ensuring that products, services, and processes consistently meet established standards and exceed customer expectations. It encompasses planning, control, assurance, and continuous improvement strategies to maintain high-quality outcomes. Key components include setting quality objectives, monitoring production processes, identifying defects, and implementing corrective actions. Techniques like Total Quality Management (TQM) and Six Sigma are often applied to enhance efficiency, reduce waste, and foster a culture of excellence. By prioritizing quality management, organizations can improve customer satisfaction, strengthen brand reputation, and achieve long-term success in competitive markets.

- Implementing Total Quality Management (TQM) and Six Sigma methodologies
- Ensuring product and process quality through continuous improvement

4. Operations Research: Operations research is a discipline that utilizes mathematical models and optimization techniques to make better decisions and solve complex problems. By applying mathematical models, operations researchers can represent real-world systems and processes, allowing them to analyze different scenarios and predict outcomes. Optimization techniques, such as linear programming and integer programming, help in finding the most efficient solutions to problems involving resource allocation, scheduling, and logistics. Additionally, operations research involves conducting simulations to model and study the behavior of systems under various conditions. Through simulation, researchers can test different strategies and identify potential improvements without disrupting actual operations. Decision analysis is another crucial aspect, where quantitative methods are used to evaluate and compare different decision options, considering factors such as risk, uncertainty, and trade-offs. Together, these approaches enable organizations to enhance productivity, reduce costs, and improve overall effectiveness in their operations. Operations research is a discipline that applies advanced analytical methods to help organizations make better decisions and solve complex problems. It uses techniques such as mathematical modeling, statistical analysis, and optimization to evaluate various scenarios and identify the most efficient and effective solutions. Common applications include optimizing supply chain management, scheduling, resource allocation, and risk assessment. By providing data-driven insights, operations research enables industries to enhance productivity, reduce costs, and improve decision-making processes, making it an essential tool for tackling challenges in both manufacturing and service sectors.

- Applying mathematical models and optimization techniques
- Conducting simulation and decision analysis

5. Supply Chain Management: Supply chain management is a critical discipline that involves designing and optimizing supply chain networks to ensure the smooth flow of goods, information, and finances from suppliers to customers. This process begins with strategic planning to determine the optimal configuration of the supply chain, including the location and capacity of manufacturing facilities, warehouses, and distribution centers. By analyzing various factors such as demand patterns, transportation costs, and lead times, businesses can create an efficient and resilient supply chain network. Managing logistics and distribution effectively is another essential aspect, which entails coordinating transportation, inventory management, and order fulfillment to meet customer demands in a timely and cost-effective manner. Advanced technologies like real-time tracking, route optimization, and automation play a crucial role in enhancing the efficiency and reliability of logistics operations. Overall, effective supply chain management ensures that products are delivered to the right place, at the right time, and at the right cost, ultimately enhancing customer satisfaction and business performance. Supply chain management (SCM) is the coordination and oversight of the flow of goods, services, information, and finances across all stages of production, from raw material sourcing to delivering the final product to consumers. It involves optimizing processes such as procurement, inventory management, transportation, and distribution to ensure efficiency and cost-effectiveness. Effective SCM focuses on building strong supplier relationships, adopting technology for real-time tracking, and implementing strategies to minimize waste and delays. By enhancing visibility and collaboration across the supply chain, organizations can meet customer demands, reduce operational costs, and achieve a competitive advantage in the marketplace.

- Designing and optimizing supply chain networks
- Managing logistics and distribution effectively

6. Information Systems: Information systems play a pivotal role in modern industrial processes by harnessing the power of IT and automation to enhance efficiency and productivity. By integrating various technologies, such as enterprise resource planning (ERP) systems and manufacturing execution systems (MES), information systems enable seamless communication and coordination across different departments. Automation technologies, including robotics and IoT devices, streamline operations by performing repetitive tasks with precision and speed, reducing the need for manual intervention. Furthermore, information systems facilitate data collection and analysis, providing valuable insights for informed decision-making. Advanced data analytics tools process vast amounts of data generated by industrial processes, identifying patterns and trends that can optimize resource allocation, improve quality control, and drive innovation. Ultimately, information systems serve as the backbone of industrial operations, enabling organizations to remain competitive in an increasingly data-driven and automated world. Information systems refer to the structured combination of hardware, software, data, and processes used to collect, manage, and analyze information to support decision-making and operations within an organization. These systems play a vital role in improving efficiency, enhancing communication, and streamlining workflows by providing real-time access to critical data. In manufacturing and industrial settings, information systems are used for tasks such as inventory management, production planning, quality control, and supply chain optimization. By leveraging advanced technologies like cloud computing, artificial intelligence, and data analytics, information systems enable organizations to adapt to changing demands, improve productivity, and maintain a competitive edge in the modern business landscape.

- Utilizing IT and automation in industrial processes
- Analyzing data for informed decision-making

7. Sustainability and Green Manufacturing: Sustainability and green manufacturing are essential approaches that focus on promoting environmentally responsible practices to minimize the ecological footprint of industrial activities. This involves adopting sustainable practices that reduce environmental impact by conserving resources, minimizing waste, and lowering emissions. Companies implement eco-friendly processes such as recycling, using renewable energy sources, and selecting sustainable materials to ensure that their operations are not only efficient but also environmentally conscious. Additionally, energy-efficient technologies, such as energy-saving machinery and optimized production methods, are utilized to decrease energy consumption and reduce greenhouse gas emissions. By integrating these principles, green manufacturing not only helps preserve the environment but also enhances the long-term viability of businesses by reducing operational costs and meeting the growing demand for sustainable products. Through continuous improvement and innovation, industries can achieve a balance between economic growth and environmental stewardship, contributing to a sustainable future. Sustainability and green manufacturing are essential approaches focused on minimizing environmental impact while maintaining industrial productivity. Sustainability involves adopting practices that conserve resources, reduce emissions, and promote long-term ecological balance. Green manufacturing implements these principles by using energy-efficient technologies, renewable energy sources, and sustainable materials, along with waste reduction strategies such as recycling and reuse. It emphasizes eco-friendly product design and cleaner production processes that prioritize environmental well-being. By integrating sustainability and green manufacturing, industries can enhance efficiency, reduce costs, and contribute to a healthier planet while meeting consumer demand for environmentally responsible products.

- Promoting sustainable practices and reducing environmental impact
- Implementing energy-efficient and eco-friendly processes

8. Human Factors and Safety Engineering: Human factors and safety engineering are disciplines dedicated to enhancing safety and minimizing risks in the workplace by considering the interactions between humans and systems. By analyzing human behavior, capabilities, and limitations, these fields aim to design systems and work environments that promote safety, efficiency, and well-being. This involves incorporating ergonomic principles to create comfortable and user-friendly workstations, ensuring that tools and equipment are designed to fit the natural movements and abilities of workers. Safety engineering also focuses on identifying potential hazards, conducting risk assessments, and implementing preventive measures to mitigate risks. By integrating human factors into system design and operation, organizations can reduce the likelihood of accidents, improve overall safety, and enhance worker productivity. Through continuous evaluation and improvement, human factors and safety engineering contribute to creating safer, more efficient, and more satisfying work environments for employees. Human factors and safety engineering is a discipline that focuses on designing systems, processes, and environments that prioritize the well-being, efficiency, and safety of individuals. It involves understanding human capabilities and limitations to ensure that tools, equipment, and workplaces are user-friendly and reduce the risk of errors or accidents. By integrating ergonomic principles, cognitive psychology, and risk assessment, this field aims to create safer and more effective work systems. Safety engineering specifically addresses hazard identification, risk mitigation, and compliance with safety standards to protect workers and prevent accidents. Together, human factors and safety engineering contribute to enhancing productivity, reducing workplace injuries, and promoting a culture of safety and well-being across industries.

- Enhancing safety and minimizing risks in the workplace
- Considering human factors in system design and operation

Industrial Engineers work in various sectors, including manufacturing, healthcare, logistics, finance, and more. Their expertise is crucial in achieving operational excellence and driving innovation in today's competitive and dynamic industries.

CHAPTER TWO

History and Evolution

Industrial Engineering has a rich history that traces its roots back to the Industrial Revolution in the late 18th century. Initially, it emerged as a response to the need for systematic study and improvement of work processes during the shift from handcraft to mechanized production. The early 20th century marked significant advancements with the introduction of scientific management by Frederick Winslow Taylor, emphasizing time and motion studies for increased productivity. The Human Relations Movement in the 1920s and 1930s further highlighted the importance of worker satisfaction and human factors. World War II saw the development of operations research, focusing on efficient resource allocation and logistics. Post-war, industrial engineering principles were widely applied across industries, including quality management and supply chain optimization. The latter half of the 20th century brought Total Quality Management (TQM) and Lean Manufacturing, promoting waste reduction and quality improvement. Technological advancements in computers and automation revolutionized the field, integrating IT and data analytics into industrial processes. Today, industrial engineering continues to evolve with advancements in artificial intelligence, the Industrial Internet of Things (IIoT), and sustainable practices, driving innovation and efficiency in various industries.

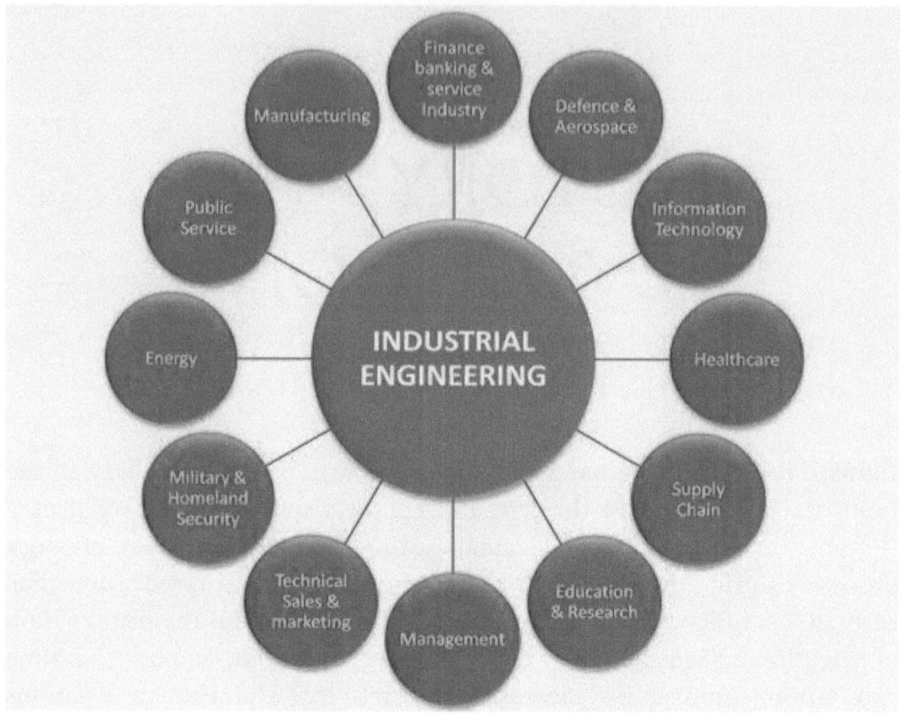

Industrial Engineering

Industrial Engineering has a rich history, tracing its origins back to the early days of the Industrial Revolution. Here's a brief overview of its evolution:

1. Early Beginnings:

The origins of industrial engineering trace back to the late 18th century, during the transformative period known as the Industrial Revolution. This era marked a significant transition from traditional handcraft methods to mechanized production, driven by the advent of new machinery and manufacturing techniques. As factories began to emerge, there was a growing need to optimize these new production processes to improve efficiency, reduce costs, and enhance productivity. Early pioneers in this field, such as Frederick Winslow Taylor and Henry Ford, recognized the importance of systematically studying work processes. Taylor's principles of scientific management focused on analyzing tasks to develop the most efficient ways of performing them, while Ford's assembly line revolutionized mass production by standardizing and streamlining workflows. These early efforts laid the foundation for industrial engineering, setting the stage for the development of methods and principles that continue to shape modern manufacturing and operations management. The emphasis on systematic analysis, process improvement, and efficiency remains at the core of industrial engineering, driving innovation and progress in various industries.

2. Scientific Management:

The early 20th century marked a pivotal era in the evolution of industrial engineering with the advent of scientific management, a groundbreaking approach spearheaded by Frederick Winslow Taylor. Taylor's philosophy centered on the systematic study of work processes to enhance productivity and efficiency. He introduced time and motion studies, meticulously analyzing the tasks performed by workers to identify the most efficient ways to complete them. By breaking down tasks into their fundamental components, Taylor was able to eliminate unnecessary movements and streamline workflows. This method led to the development of standardized work practices and the implementation of best practices across various industries. Taylor's principles of scientific management emphasized the importance of training workers, providing them with the right tools and techniques, and incentivizing performance through fair compensation. His approach revolutionized manufacturing, leading to significant improvements in productivity and setting the foundation for modern industrial engineering practices. Taylor's legacy continues to influence contemporary management theories and practices, underscoring the enduring relevance of scientific management in optimizing work methods and enhancing organizational efficiency.

3. Human Relations Movement:

The 1920s and 1930s heralded a transformative period in industrial engineering with the emergence of the Human Relations Movement, significantly influenced by Elton Mayo and the seminal Hawthorne Studies. This movement marked a departure from the purely mechanistic approaches of earlier management theories by highlighting the profound impact of human factors on workplace productivity. The Hawthorne Studies, conducted at the Western Electric Hawthorne Works, revealed that social and psychological factors, such as employee satisfaction, group dynamics, and a sense of belonging, played a crucial role in influencing workers' performance. These studies demonstrated that employees were not just motivated by monetary incentives and optimal working conditions but also by intangible elements like recognition, communication, and involvement in decision-making processes. This recognition led to a greater emphasis on fostering positive workplace environments, improving employee relations, and addressing the emotional and social needs of workers. The Human Relations Movement laid the groundwork for modern human resources practices and underscored the importance of considering the holistic well-being of employees to achieve sustainable productivity and organizational success.

4. World War II and Operations Research:

World War II was a catalyst for significant advancements in the field of operations research, driven by the urgent need for efficient resource allocation and logistics in the face of complex military challenges. During this period, mathematicians, engineers, and scientists were called upon to apply analytical methods to optimize the use of limited resources, enhance strategic planning, and improve decision-making processes. Techniques such as linear programming, queuing theory, and simulation were developed and employed to address critical issues, including troop deployment, supply chain management, and the optimal allocation of equipment. These pioneering efforts in operations research not only contributed to the success of military operations but also laid the foundation for modern industrial engineering practices. The systematic and quantitative approaches developed during the war have since been adapted and refined for use in various industries, leading to significant improvements in efficiency, productivity, and overall operational effectiveness. The legacy of World War II operations research continues to influence contemporary industrial engineering, demonstrating the enduring impact of these early innovations on the field.

5. Post-War Expansion:

Following World War II, industrial engineering experienced significant expansion as its principles and practices were applied across various industries, including manufacturing, healthcare, and logistics. The rapid post-war industrial growth and the need for efficient production processes led to the widespread adoption of industrial engineering techniques. In manufacturing, industrial engineers focused on streamlining production lines, optimizing resource allocation, and implementing quality management systems to ensure consistent product quality. The healthcare sector began to benefit from industrial engineering through improved hospital management, patient flow optimization, and the implementation of efficient scheduling systems. In logistics, the principles of supply chain management and optimization were employed to enhance the efficiency of transportation networks, inventory management, and distribution systems. This era also saw the integration of advanced technologies and analytical methods, such as operations research and statistical process control, further enhancing the effectiveness of industrial engineering practices. Overall, the post-war period marked a transformative phase in the field, with industrial engineering principles driving innovation, productivity, and efficiency across diverse industries, setting the stage for modern operational excellence.

6. Total Quality Management and Lean Manufacturing:

In the latter half of the 20th century, Total Quality Management (TQM) and Lean Manufacturing emerged as pivotal methodologies in the industrial and business sectors. Total Quality Management (TQM) introduced a holistic approach to long-term success through customer satisfaction, focusing on continuous improvement in all aspects of an organization. By involving every employee, from top management to frontline workers, TQM emphasized process-driven improvement, quality control, and the integration of quality into every step of production and service delivery. This customer-centric philosophy sought not just to meet but to exceed customer expectations by fostering a culture of quality awareness and proactive problem-solving.

Meanwhile, Lean Manufacturing, pioneered by Toyota, revolutionized production processes by targeting waste elimination and optimizing resource utilization. Lean principles, encapsulated in techniques such as Just-In-Time (JIT) production, Kanban systems, and value stream mapping, aimed to streamline operations, reduce cycle times, and enhance overall efficiency. By focusing on value-adding activities and minimizing non-value-adding steps, Lean Manufacturing sought to deliver high-quality products at lower costs while maintaining flexibility and responsiveness to market demands. Together, TQM and Lean Manufacturing have profoundly influenced industries worldwide, driving significant improvements in quality, efficiency, and customer satisfaction, and setting new benchmarks for operational excellence.

7. Technological Advancements:

The advent of computers and automation in the late 20th century brought about a transformative revolution in industrial engineering. The integration of information systems allowed for the seamless management of vast amounts of data, facilitating real-time tracking, analysis, and decision-making across various industrial processes. Data analytics emerged as a powerful tool, enabling engineers to uncover patterns, predict trends, and optimize operations with unprecedented precision. Automation technologies, including robotics and automated control systems, significantly enhanced efficiency by performing repetitive and complex tasks with high accuracy and speed. These advancements collectively enabled industries to achieve higher levels of productivity, reduce operational costs, and improve quality. The implementation of computer-aided design (CAD) and computer-aided manufacturing (CAM) further streamlined product development and manufacturing processes, allowing for greater innovation and customization. Overall, the technological advancements of this era not only revolutionized industrial engineering but also laid the foundation for the modern, interconnected, and highly efficient industrial landscape we see today.

8. Modern Era and Future Trends:

Today, industrial engineering continues to evolve with advancements in artificial intelligence, the Industrial Internet of Things (IIoT), and data-driven decision-making. The focus is on sustainable practices, smart manufacturing, and the integration of cutting-edge technologies to drive innovation and efficiency.

Industrial Engineering has come a long way from its early beginnings, continuously adapting to the changing needs of industries and society. Its principles and methodologies remain vital in addressing the challenges of modern production and operations.

CHAPTER THREE

SYSTEMS APPROACH

The systems approach in industrial engineering is a holistic method that focuses on optimizing the performance of complex systems by considering the interactions and interdependencies of all components. Instead of analyzing parts in isolation, it emphasizes understanding the entire system to ensure improvements in one area do not negatively affect others. This interdisciplinary approach involves collaboration with professionals from various fields and aims to achieve the best balance between objectives such as cost, quality, and efficiency. By incorporating feedback loops and integrating subsystems, the systems approach enhances overall performance, efficiency, and adaptability. It is widely applied across industries, including manufacturing, healthcare, supply chain management, and transportation, to drive innovation and operational excellence.

The systems approach is a holistic and interdisciplinary method used in industrial engineering to analyze, design, and manage complex systems. This approach focuses on understanding the interactions and interdependencies within a system to optimize its overall performance. Here's a brief overview:

Key Principles:

1. **Holistic View:** The systems approach considers the entire system, rather than focusing on individual components in isolation. This ensures that improvements in one area do not negatively impact other parts of the system. By adopting a comprehensive perspective, industrial engineers can identify and address potential inefficiencies, conflicts, or unintended consequences that might arise when changes are made. This holistic view promotes harmonious integration of all elements within the system, leading to optimized overall performance and sustainable

improvements.

2. **Interdisciplinary Collaboration:** Industrial engineers often work with professionals from various fields, such as mechanical engineering, operations research, economics, and psychology, to develop comprehensive solutions. This collaboration allows for the integration of diverse perspectives, expertise, and methodologies, leading to more innovative and effective outcomes. By leveraging the strengths of different disciplines, industrial engineers can address complex challenges, optimize processes, and create systems that are not only efficient but also adaptable to changing conditions and requirements. This interdisciplinary approach is essential for achieving holistic and sustainable improvements in various industries.
3. **Optimization:** The goal is to optimize the system's performance by finding the best balance between competing objectives, such as cost, quality, and efficiency. Industrial engineers use various techniques and tools to identify inefficiencies, streamline processes, and enhance productivity. This involves analyzing data, modeling scenarios, and implementing changes that lead to the optimal functioning of the entire system. The optimization process ensures that resources are used effectively, waste is minimized, and the desired outcomes are achieved without compromising on quality or performance. Through continuous monitoring and improvement, industrial engineers strive to maintain this balance and drive sustainable growth in the system.
4. **Feedback Loops:** Understanding and incorporating feedback loops within the system is crucial for continuous improvement and adaptation to changing conditions. Feedback loops provide essential information on the system's performance, allowing for real-time adjustments and ongoing optimization. By analyzing feedback, industrial engineers can identify areas that need improvement, implement changes, and monitor the outcomes. This iterative process ensures that the system remains efficient and responsive to new challenges, ultimately enhancing overall performance and achieving long-term success.
5. **Integration:** Systems approach emphasizes the integration of various subsystems, ensuring that all components work seamlessly together to achieve the desired outcomes. By coordinating and aligning the functions of each subsystem, industrial engineers can create a cohesive and efficient system. This integration fosters collaboration, minimizes conflicts, and enhances the overall performance. It ensures that every

part of the system contributes to the common goals, leading to optimized processes, improved productivity, and successful achievement of desired results.

Applications:

Manufacturing: Designing efficient production lines, improving workflow, and reducing waste through lean manufacturing principles. Industrial engineers apply these principles to streamline production processes, minimize inefficiencies, and enhance productivity. By carefully analyzing each step of the manufacturing process, they identify areas for improvement and implement strategies to eliminate waste. This approach leads to cost savings, improved product quality, and a more efficient use of resources, ultimately contributing to the overall success of the manufacturing operation.

Manufacturing is the process of transforming raw materials into finished products on a large scale, leveraging advanced machinery, skilled labor, and innovative technologies. It serves as the backbone of industrial economies, driving progress, innovation, and growth. Modern manufacturing integrates sustainable practices, such as reducing waste, optimizing resource utilization, and adopting cleaner technologies. Designing efficient production lines, improving workflow, and enhancing output quality are essential components. Techniques like automation, robotics, and lean manufacturing principles help streamline operations, minimize inefficiencies, and reduce costs. Industrial engineers play a pivotal role in analyzing and refining every step of the production process to ensure it aligns with environmental goals and customer demands. This approach not only leads to operational excellence but also strengthens competitiveness and contributes to the overall success and sustainability of the manufacturing industry.

Supply Chain Management: Optimizing the flow of materials, information, and resources across the supply chain to enhance overall performance. Industrial engineers focus on designing and managing supply chain networks to ensure efficient movement of goods from suppliers to customers. This involves improving logistics, reducing lead times, and minimizing costs while maintaining high levels of service and quality. By leveraging advanced technologies and data analytics, industrial engineers can create responsive and resilient supply chains that adapt to changing market demands and disruptions, ultimately driving competitive advantage and customer satisfaction.

Supply chain management (SCM) is the strategic coordination of all activities involved in the production and delivery of goods and services, ensuring seamless integration from suppliers to customers. It encompasses procurement, manufacturing, inventory management, transportation, and distribution processes, optimizing the flow of materials, information, and resources to enhance efficiency and minimize costs. Industrial engineers play a pivotal role in designing and managing supply chain networks to address challenges such as reducing lead times, improving logistics, and maintaining high-quality standards. By leveraging advanced technologies such as artificial intelligence, IoT-enabled tracking systems, and predictive analytics, supply chains are transformed into responsive and resilient ecosystems. These innovations enable businesses to adapt swiftly to changing market demands, mitigate disruptions, and maintain a competitive edge. Furthermore, sustainability practices like reducing carbon emissions and promoting eco-friendly logistics are increasingly integrated into SCM, creating value not only for businesses but also for the environment. Ultimately, effective supply chain management drives customer satisfaction, reduces operational costs, and supports long-term growth and profitability.

Healthcare: Streamlining hospital operations, improving patient flow, and enhancing the quality of care through system-wide interventions. Industrial engineers analyze healthcare processes to identify inefficiencies and bottlenecks, ensuring that resources are utilized effectively. By redesigning workflows, implementing technology solutions, and optimizing scheduling, they can enhance patient experiences and outcomes. This approach leads to reduced wait times, better resource allocation, and improved overall efficiency in healthcare facilities.

Healthcare systems are complex ecosystems requiring precise coordination to deliver high-quality care effectively. Industrial engineers play a critical role in streamlining hospital operations, improving patient flow, and ensuring efficient resource utilization. By analyzing processes such as admissions, diagnostics, and treatment pathways, they identify bottlenecks and inefficiencies that impede patient care. Through workflow redesign, technological integration, and the optimization of scheduling and staffing, they aim to enhance the overall patient experience. Implementing solutions like predictive analytics for demand forecasting, automated systems for appointment scheduling, and optimized layouts for emergency and inpatient facilities can significantly reduce wait times, improve resource allocation, and boost operational efficiency. Furthermore, by fostering collaboration between healthcare professionals and ensuring compliance with safety and quality standards, industrial engineers contribute to better patient outcomes and increased satisfaction. This systematic approach not only improves the effectiveness of individual healthcare facilities but also strengthens the resilience of the broader healthcare system.

Transportation: Developing efficient transportation networks, optimizing traffic flow, and reducing congestion through integrated planning. Industrial engineers analyze transportation systems to identify inefficiencies and design solutions that enhance mobility. By incorporating advanced technologies, data analytics, and strategic planning, they can create sustainable and efficient transportation networks. These improvements lead to reduced travel times, lower environmental impact, and better overall connectivity, contributing to the economic and social well-being of communities.

Transportation systems are vital to enabling the seamless movement of people, goods, and services, serving as the backbone of economic and social development. Industrial engineers play a key role in developing efficient transportation networks by carefully analyzing existing systems to identify inefficiencies, bottlenecks, and areas for improvement. Through integrated planning and data-driven decision-making, they design solutions aimed at optimizing traffic flow and reducing congestion. Incorporating advanced technologies such as artificial intelligence, GPS-based tracking systems, and predictive modeling allows them to enhance route planning, monitor real-time conditions, and adapt to changing demands. Additionally, the adoption of sustainable practices, including promoting public transportation, reducing reliance on fossil fuels, and encouraging eco-friendly transit options, helps lower environmental impact. These strategies not only reduce travel times and improve overall connectivity but also contribute to the long-term resilience and well-being of communities, supporting urban development and economic growth in a rapidly evolving world.

Project Management:

Coordinating complex projects by ensuring that all components and stakeholders are aligned towards common goals. Industrial engineers use project management techniques to plan, execute, and monitor projects efficiently. By defining clear objectives, setting timelines, and managing resources, they ensure that projects are completed on time and within budget. Effective communication and collaboration among team members are essential to address challenges and achieve desired outcomes. This approach helps in delivering successful projects that meet the expectations of all stakeholders and contribute to the overall success of the organization.

Project management is a systematic approach to organizing and overseeing complex projects, ensuring that all elements are aligned with the overall objectives and completed efficiently. Industrial engineers play a vital role in this process by employing techniques to meticulously plan, execute, and monitor every stage of a project. They begin by defining clear and measurable goals, creating detailed timelines, and allocating resources effectively to maintain efficiency. Risk management is also a critical aspect, allowing for proactive identification and mitigation of potential obstacles. Strong communication strategies and collaboration among diverse teams ensure that all stakeholders remain informed and engaged, fostering a sense of unity and purpose. Utilizing tools such as Gantt charts, project management software, and data analytics, engineers are able to track progress and adapt to changes as needed. This structured approach not only ensures projects are completed on time and within budget but also upholds high standards of quality and achieves results that satisfy stakeholders' expectations, driving organizational success and long-term growth.

Benefits:

Improved Efficiency:

By considering the entire system, industrial engineers can identify and eliminate inefficiencies that might be overlooked when focusing on individual components. This holistic approach ensures that all aspects of the system work harmoniously together, leading to optimized processes, reduced waste, and enhanced productivity. By addressing inefficiencies at a systemic level, industrial engineers can achieve significant improvements in overall performance, resulting in cost savings and better resource utilization.

Improved efficiency is achieved through a comprehensive evaluation of entire systems rather than isolated components, allowing industrial engineers to uncover inefficiencies that might otherwise go unnoticed. By taking a holistic approach, they ensure that each element of the system functions in alignment, creating a seamless workflow that eliminates redundancies, reduces delays, and maximizes resource utilization. This systemic perspective enables the identification of bottlenecks, wasteful practices, and underutilized assets, facilitating the implementation of innovative solutions that enhance overall productivity. Through techniques such as process reengineering, automation, and real-time monitoring, industrial engineers can achieve substantial performance improvements. These enhancements translate into not only cost savings and optimized resource allocation but also increased operational agility, enabling organizations to adapt to changing demands and maintain a competitive edge in dynamic markets. Ultimately, addressing inefficiencies at the system level leads to sustainable growth and long-term success.

Enhanced Quality:

A holistic view helps in maintaining high-quality standards across all aspects of the system. By considering the entire system, industrial engineers can ensure that quality is consistently achieved and maintained in every component and process. This comprehensive approach enables the identification and mitigation of potential issues before they impact the final product or service. It also promotes continuous improvement, leading to superior quality outcomes and increased customer satisfaction.

Enhanced quality is achieved by adopting a holistic approach that ensures high standards are upheld across all facets of a system, from design and production to delivery and support. Industrial engineers play a pivotal role in maintaining consistency by thoroughly analyzing processes, components, and workflows to identify and address potential issues early, preventing defects or inefficiencies from compromising the final product or service. This proactive strategy involves integrating quality assurance practices, utilizing advanced monitoring technologies, and implementing feedback loops that drive continuous improvement. By fostering collaboration among stakeholders and encouraging adherence to quality protocols, the entire system works harmoniously to produce superior outcomes. The commitment to enhanced quality not only strengthens customer trust and loyalty but also supports long-term success by enabling organizations to exceed expectations and remain competitive in a rapidly evolving market landscape.

Cost Savings:

Optimizing the system as a whole can lead to significant cost reductions through better resource utilization and waste minimization. By considering all aspects of the system, industrial engineers can identify opportunities to streamline processes, reduce redundancies, and eliminate waste. This holistic approach ensures that resources are allocated efficiently, leading to lower operational costs. The resulting cost savings can be reinvested in other areas of the organization, driving further innovation and growth.

Cost savings is a crucial benefit of system optimization, achieved by carefully analyzing and improving every aspect of operations to maximize efficiency and minimize waste. Industrial engineers employ a strategic, system-wide perspective to identify inefficiencies, redundancies, and underutilized resources across processes and workflows. By integrating innovative technologies, such as automation and data-driven decision-making, they can further refine operations to reduce errors and energy consumption. This leads to significant reductions in overhead costs and better allocation of financial and material resources. Additionally, optimized systems often result in improved product quality and faster delivery times, which can enhance customer satisfaction and boost revenue. The savings generated from these improvements can be redirected to key areas such as research and development, employee training, and technological advancements, fostering a cycle of continuous innovation and growth that strengthens the organization's competitive edge in the market.

Adaptability:

The systems approach allows for better adaptation to changing conditions and continuous improvement through feedback loops. By continuously monitoring system performance and incorporating feedback, industrial engineers can identify areas for improvement and make necessary adjustments. This dynamic process ensures that the system remains responsive to new challenges and opportunities, ultimately enhancing its efficiency and effectiveness over time. The ability to adapt and evolve is crucial for maintaining a competitive edge in a rapidly changing environment.

The systems approach is a fundamental concept in industrial engineering, enabling engineers to tackle complex challenges and develop innovative solutions that enhance overall system performance. By considering the entire system and understanding the interactions between its components, engineers can optimize processes, improve efficiency, and ensure sustainable and effective solutions. This holistic view allows for better resource utilization, adaptability to changing conditions, and continuous improvement, ultimately driving innovation and excellence in various industries.

CHAPTER FOUR

Optimization and Efficiency

Optimization in industrial engineering is a critical practice that focuses on improving and streamlining processes to achieve maximum efficiency and effectiveness. It involves the application of various mathematical and computational techniques to determine the best possible solutions for complex industrial problems. Efficiency, in this context, pertains to the optimal use of resources, such as time, labor, and materials, to minimize waste and maximize productivity.

In industrial engineering, optimization can be applied to a wide range of areas, including production planning, supply chain management, inventory control, and quality assurance. For instance, linear programming is commonly used to allocate resources in a way that meets production targets while minimizing costs. Non-linear programming, on the other hand, addresses more complex problems where relationships between variables are not linear. Integer programming and combinatorial optimization are useful for decision-making in situations involving discrete choices, such as scheduling and routing.

Heuristic and metaheuristic methods, such as genetic algorithms and simulated annealing, offer robust solutions for problems that are difficult to solve using traditional optimization techniques. These methods are particularly valuable when dealing with large-scale industrial problems with numerous variables and constraints.

Moreover, multi-criteria optimization is essential in scenarios where multiple objectives must be balanced, such as maximizing production efficiency while minimizing environmental impact. Stochastic optimization addresses uncertainty in industrial processes by incorporating probabilistic elements into the optimization model, ensuring that solutions are robust and reliable.

Real-world applications of optimization in industrial engineering are vast. Supply chain management benefits from optimization techniques to improve logistics and reduce lead times. Production planning and scheduling utilize optimization to enhance process efficiency and meet demand fluctuations. Inventory management applies optimization to maintain optimal stock levels and reduce holding costs. Quality control and improvement initiatives use optimization to achieve consistent product quality and reduce defects.

Looking ahead, emerging technologies such as artificial intelligence, machine learning, and the Internet of Things (IoT) are poised to revolutionize optimization in industrial engineering. These technologies enable more sophisticated and dynamic optimization models, offering new opportunities for efficiency gains and innovation in industrial processes.

In summary, optimization and efficiency are foundational concepts in industrial engineering that drive continuous improvement and innovation. By leveraging advanced optimization techniques and embracing new technologies, industrial engineers can tackle complex challenges and enhance the performance of industrial systems.

Efficiency in industrial engineering is the cornerstone of optimizing processes, reducing waste, and maximizing productivity. It involves the strategic use of resources such as time, labor, and materials to achieve the best possible outcomes with minimal input. By implementing efficiency-enhancing techniques, industrial engineers can streamline production processes, improve supply chain management, and ensure that operations run smoothly and cost-effectively. This not only leads to significant cost savings but also enhances overall performance and competitiveness in the market. Efficiency is achieved through various methods, including lean manufacturing, Six Sigma, and continuous improvement practices, which focus on identifying and eliminating inefficiencies, thus ensuring a more agile and responsive industrial environment. Ultimately, the pursuit of efficiency drives innovation and fosters a culture of excellence within organizations.

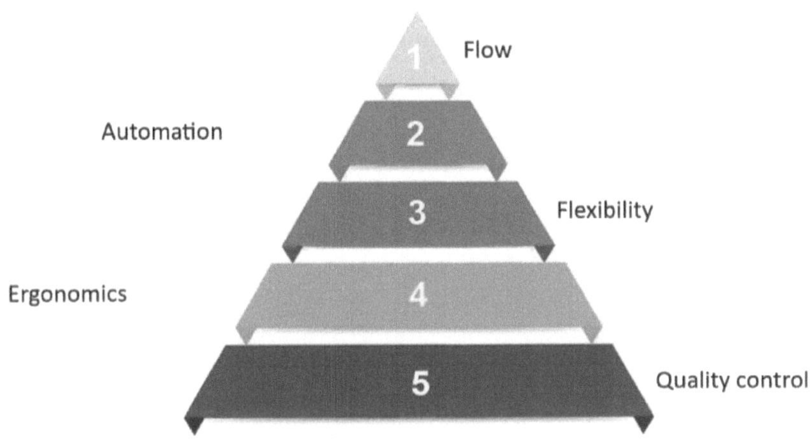

Assembly Line Design and Optimization for Efficiency

1. Automation

Industrial engineers focus on integrating technologies like robotics, computer-aided manufacturing (CAM), and IoT devices to maximize efficiency and reduce manual intervention.

2. Ergonomics

Designing workstations that cater to human factors is critical. Industrial engineers employ ergonomic assessments to prevent workplace injuries and improve operator efficiency and satisfaction.

3. Flow

Through techniques like process mapping, time-motion studies, and lean manufacturing principles, industrial engineers ensure that tasks are synchronized and bottlenecks are eliminated.

4. Flexibility

Industrial engineering promotes adaptable systems by implementing modular designs, universal tools, and rapid changeover methods to cater to diverse production demands.

5. Quality Control

Continuous improvement methods, such as Six Sigma and statistical process control, are integral to industrial engineering to ensure that products meet high-quality standards consistently.

CHAPTER FIVE

TIME AND MOTION STUDY

Time and Motion Study is a crucial technique in industrial engineering used to analyze work processes and enhance efficiency. This method involves observing, measuring, and recording the time taken to perform specific tasks and the motions involved in these tasks. The main objective is to identify and eliminate unnecessary or redundant movements, streamline workflows, and establish standardized procedures.

Time Study focuses on measuring the duration of each task element, aiming to set time standards and improve task performance. Motion Study, on the other hand, examines the movements of workers and machines to identify the most efficient ways to perform tasks with minimal physical strain and effort.

By combining Time and Motion Studies, industrial engineers can develop more effective work methods, reduce production costs, increase productivity, and improve worker safety and comfort. The insights gained from these studies help in designing ergonomic workstations, optimizing labor allocation, and enhancing overall operational efficiency.

In practice, Time and Motion Studies have been widely applied across various industries, from manufacturing and logistics to healthcare and service sectors. Their impact on productivity and efficiency continues to be significant, driving continuous improvement and operational excellence in modern industrial settings.

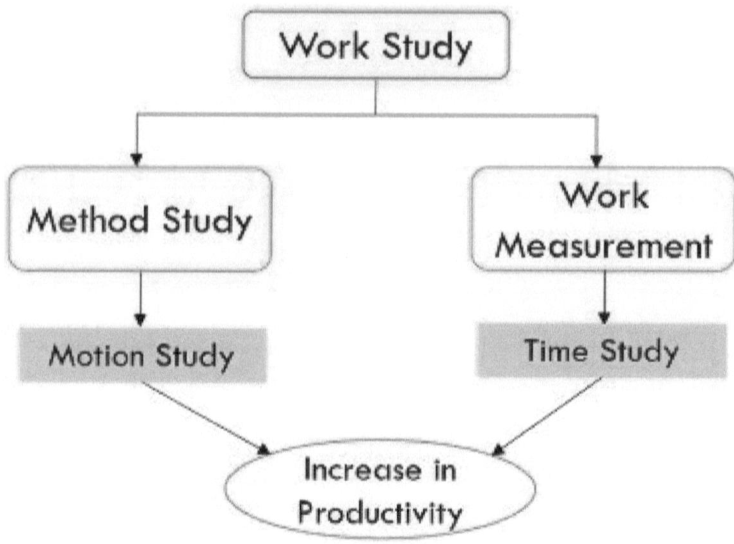

Time and Motion Study

Time and Motion Study is a systematic approach to analyzing work processes to improve efficiency and productivity. It involves examining how tasks are performed (method study), measuring the time taken for each activity (time study), and optimizing workers' movements (motion study) to eliminate unnecessary effort and enhance ergonomics. Work measurement establishes standard times, ensuring balanced workloads and fair task distribution. These studies collectively help organizations reduce waste, streamline workflows, and boost output while maintaining quality and worker satisfaction. By refining processes, industrial engineers achieve significant increases in overall productivity and operational efficiency.

1. Work Study

This is the overarching term that encompasses both method study and work measurement. It focuses on evaluating processes to enhance efficiency while maintaining quality standards.

2. Method Study

It involves analyzing the way tasks are performed and identifying opportunities to simplify or eliminate unnecessary actions. Tools like flowcharts and process mapping are commonly used for this purpose.

3. Work Measurement

Work measurement quantifies the time required to complete tasks. Techniques like stopwatch time study, predetermined motion-time systems, and synthesis are used to establish standard times and ensure fair workloads.

4. Motion Study

Motion study examines the movements made by workers during a task. Its goal is to optimize motions by reducing wasteful movements and improving ergonomics, thereby enhancing speed and comfort.

5. Time Study

Time study uses a stopwatch to measure the duration of each task performed. It helps in setting benchmarks and identifying areas for improvement in cycle times.

6. Increase in Productivity

By combining insights from these studies, organizations can:

- Minimize waste and unnecessary effort.
- Improve workflow and task efficiency.
- Enhance worker satisfaction through better ergonomics and fair time allocations.
- Achieve higher output with consistent quality.

Example 1: Automobile Assembly Line

In an automotive manufacturing plant, engineers conduct a method study to identify unnecessary steps in assembling a car. For instance, they might find that workers walk back and forth to retrieve tools, slowing production. By introducing a conveyor belt system and placing tools within arm's reach, they streamline workflow and eliminate wasted motion. Time studies ensure each workstation achieves optimal cycle times without overloading the workers, leading to increased output and reduced fatigue.

Example 2: Healthcare Operations

In a hospital setting, Time and Motion Studies are used to improve patient care processes. For example, in an emergency department, engineers analyze nurses‘ and doctors' movements to reduce the time spent fetching medical supplies. By repositioning storage rooms closer to patient areas and standardizing the arrangement of supplies, they enhance efficiency and reduce response times, ultimately improving patient outcomes.

CHAPTER SIX

Ergonomic Design and Human Factors

Ergonomic design and human factors are essential considerations in industrial engineering, aiming to create work environments that enhance human well-being and overall system performance. Ergonomics focuses on designing tools, equipment, and workspaces that align with the physical capabilities and limitations of workers. The goal is to reduce physical strain, prevent injuries, and increase comfort and efficiency.

Human factors, on the other hand, delve into the cognitive, psychological, and social aspects of human interaction with systems and environments. This includes understanding how people perceive information, make decisions, and interact with technology. By integrating human factors into design processes, engineers can create user-friendly systems that enhance productivity, safety, and user satisfaction.

Together, ergonomic design and human factors address a wide range of issues, such as reducing repetitive strain injuries, improving task performance, minimizing human errors, and promoting overall health and well-being in the workplace. By prioritizing these principles, industrial engineers can create more efficient, safer, and user-centric work environments that benefit both employees and organizations.

Ergonomic Design and Human Factors

CHAPTER SEVEN

Forecasting and Demand Planning

Forecasting and demand planning are critical components of industrial engineering, aimed at predicting future demand for products and services to ensure optimal resource allocation and production planning. Accurate forecasting helps organizations anticipate market trends, manage inventory levels, and align production schedules with customer needs.

Forecasting involves the use of historical data, statistical models, and market analysis to predict future demand. Techniques such as time series analysis, regression models, and machine learning algorithms are commonly used to generate forecasts. The goal is to identify patterns and trends that can inform decision-making and strategic planning.

Demand planning, on the other hand, focuses on aligning supply chain operations with forecasted demand. It involves collaboration across various departments, including sales, marketing, production, and logistics, to develop a comprehensive plan that meets customer requirements while minimizing costs. Demand planning includes activities such as inventory management, production scheduling, and capacity planning.

Effective forecasting and demand planning enable organizations to respond proactively to market changes, reduce stockouts and overstock situations, and improve overall operational efficiency. By leveraging advanced analytics and technology, industrial engineers can enhance the accuracy of forecasts and develop robust demand planning strategies that drive business success.

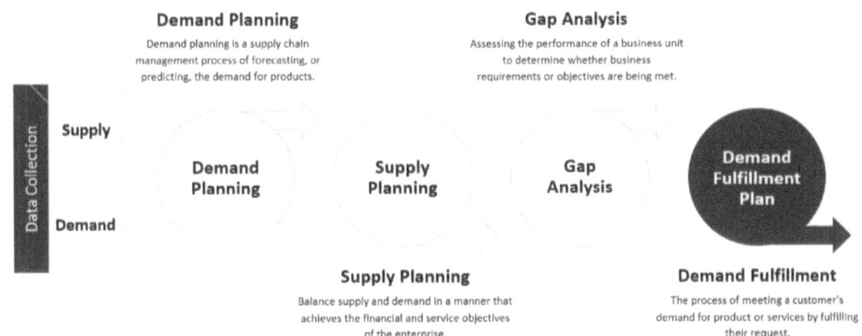

Forecasting and Demand Planning

Forecasting and Demand Planning are critical aspects of industrial engineering to ensure that production aligns with market needs and operational efficiency.

Here's an overview of the key components:

1. Demand Planning

This involves predicting future customer demand using historical data, market trends, and statistical techniques. Effective demand planning enables businesses to:

- Avoid overproduction or underproduction.
- Optimize inventory levels.
- Respond proactively to market fluctuations. For example, in the electronics industry, forecasting seasonal demand for gadgets helps manage production schedules and inventory efficiently.

2. Supply Planning

Supply planning focuses on ensuring that resources, materials, and production capacity meet the forecasted demand. It includes:

- Allocating resources across the supply chain.
- Planning procurement and manufacturing schedules.
- Managing supplier relationships to avoid disruptions. For instance, in the automotive industry, supply planning ensures a steady flow of raw materials like steel and components such as engines to meet vehicle

assembly targets.

3. Gap Analysis

Gap analysis compares the forecasted demand with the supply capability to identify mismatches. By understanding these gaps, businesses can:

- Address potential shortages or surpluses.
- Invest in capacity expansion or adjust procurement plans.
- Enhance flexibility to meet unexpected demand shifts. For example, a clothing manufacturer might perform a gap analysis to ensure they have enough fabric and skilled labor to meet a sudden spike in orders during the festive season.

CHAPTER EIGHT

Inventory Management

Inventory management is a critical component of industrial engineering, dedicated to efficiently overseeing the flow of goods and materials within an organization. Its primary objective is to strike a delicate balance between supply and demand by ensuring that the right amount of inventory is available at the right time to meet customer needs. Effective inventory management involves meticulous planning, demand forecasting, and real-time tracking of inventory levels. By employing techniques such as Just-In-Time (JIT) inventory, organizations can minimize carrying costs associated with storing excess inventory and reduce the risk of stockouts that can lead to lost sales and dissatisfied customers. Additionally, inventory management involves implementing robust systems and technologies, such as RFID and automated inventory tracking, to maintain accurate records and streamline the replenishment process. Ultimately, successful inventory management not only enhances operational efficiency but also contributes to improved customer satisfaction and overall business performance, making it an indispensable aspect of modern industrial engineering.

Effective inventory management involves several key practices:

1. **Demand Forecasting:** Demand forecasting is a critical process in supply chain management and inventory control, aimed at accurately predicting future customer demand to ensure optimal inventory levels. By leveraging historical sales data, market trends, and various statistical and machine learning techniques, businesses can anticipate fluctuations in demand and plan their inventory accordingly. Accurate demand forecasting enables organizations to maintain just the right amount of

stock, minimizing the risks associated with stockouts and overstock situations. This not only helps in meeting customer expectations and enhancing satisfaction but also reduces carrying costs and improves cash flow. Effective demand forecasting requires continuous monitoring and adjustment, as it involves various factors such as seasonality, economic conditions, and changes in consumer behavior. By staying proactive and responsive to these dynamics, companies can make informed decisions, optimize their supply chain operations, and ultimately achieve greater efficiency and profitability.

2. **Stock Replenishment:** Stock replenishment is a crucial process in inventory management that focuses on ensuring timely restocking of goods to maintain smooth operations and avoid shortages. Effective stock replenishment strategies involve continuously monitoring inventory levels and forecasting demand to determine the optimal time and quantity for replenishment. By maintaining adequate stock levels, businesses can prevent stockouts that lead to lost sales, customer dissatisfaction, and disruptions in the supply chain. Additionally, timely replenishment helps in minimizing excess inventory, which can result in increased carrying costs and potential obsolescence. Advanced technologies, such as automated inventory tracking systems and real-time data analytics, play a vital role in streamlining the replenishment process. These tools enable businesses to respond swiftly to changes in demand and ensure that inventory is replenished efficiently. Overall, a well-executed stock replenishment strategy contributes to improved customer satisfaction, reduced operational costs, and enhanced overall business performance.
3. **Safety Stock:** Safety stock is a crucial element of inventory management designed to act as a buffer against uncertainties in demand or supply. Maintaining safety stock ensures that a company can continue to meet customer demands even when unexpected fluctuations occur, such as sudden spikes in demand or delays in supply chain deliveries. By holding a reserve of additional inventory, businesses can mitigate the risk of stockouts, which can lead to lost sales, dissatisfied customers, and disrupted operations. The appropriate level of safety stock is determined by analyzing factors such as lead time variability, demand variability, and desired service levels. Advanced forecasting techniques and data analytics are often used to calculate optimal safety stock levels, striking a balance between minimizing holding costs and maximizing service

reliability. By effectively managing safety stock, companies can enhance their responsiveness to market changes, maintain smooth operations, and ensure a consistent supply of products to their customers.

4. **Inventory Tracking:** Inventory tracking is a vital aspect of inventory management that involves keeping meticulous records of inventory levels, movements, and locations using advanced technologies and systems. Methods such as barcoding and Radio Frequency Identification (RFID) are commonly employed to automate and streamline the tracking process. Barcoding involves assigning unique barcodes to individual items, which can be scanned to record their entry, movement, and exit from inventory. RFID goes a step further by using radio waves to automatically identify and track tags attached to items, providing real-time visibility into inventory status without the need for manual scanning. Additionally, inventory management software integrates these tracking technologies, offering comprehensive platforms for monitoring and managing inventory data. This software allows businesses to maintain accurate records, generate real-time reports, and set alerts for low stock levels or discrepancies. By leveraging these technologies, companies can optimize inventory accuracy, reduce the likelihood of stockouts or overstock situations, and improve overall operational efficiency. Effective inventory tracking not only ensures seamless inventory control but also enhances decision-making and customer satisfaction by providing reliable and timely information.
5. **ABC Analysis:** ABC analysis is a strategic approach to inventory management that categorizes inventory items based on their importance and value, helping organizations prioritize their resources and efforts. In this method, items are classified into three categories: A, B, and C. A items represent the most valuable and critical inventory, typically accounting for a significant portion of the inventory value but a smaller portion of the total inventory quantity. These items require close monitoring and tight control to ensure their availability and minimize stockouts. B items hold moderate value and importance, representing a middle ground between A and C items. They are managed with a balanced approach, with less stringent controls than A items but more attention than C items. C items are the least valuable and least critical, often representing a large portion of the inventory quantity but a small portion of the inventory value. These items are managed with simpler and less intensive control measures. By implementing ABC analysis,

organizations can focus their efforts and resources on the most impactful inventory items, optimizing inventory control, reducing carrying costs, and improving overall efficiency. This prioritization ensures that the most critical items are always available while streamlining the management of less important inventory.

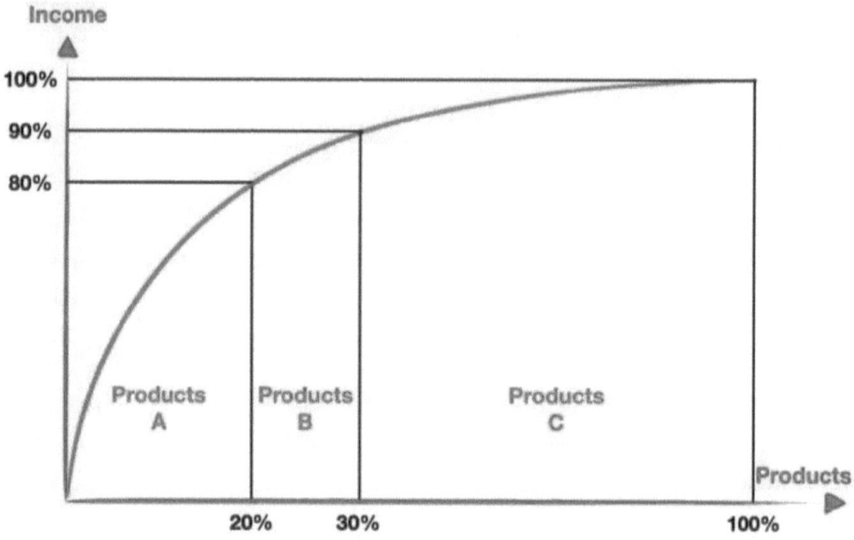

ABC Analysis

6. **Just-In-Time (JIT):** Just-In-Time (JIT) is a highly efficient inventory management strategy that aims to minimize holding costs by receiving goods only when they are needed for production or sale. By closely aligning inventory arrivals with production schedules and customer demand, JIT reduces the need for large inventory storage and minimizes the risk of overstock. This approach not only lowers carrying costs but also enhances cash flow by ensuring that capital is not tied up in excess inventory. Implementing JIT requires precise demand forecasting, strong supplier relationships, and robust communication systems to ensure timely deliveries. Additionally, JIT emphasizes lean manufacturing principles, streamlining production processes to eliminate waste and improve efficiency. By adopting JIT, companies can achieve greater flexibility in responding to market fluctuations, reduce lead times, and

enhance overall operational performance. This strategy ultimately leads to cost savings, improved productivity, and a more responsive supply chain.

7. **Economic Order Quantity (EOQ):** Economic Order Quantity (EOQ) is a fundamental inventory management concept that focuses on determining the optimal order quantity to minimize the total costs associated with inventory. These total costs comprise ordering costs, which include expenses related to placing and receiving orders, and holding costs, which encompass the costs of storing and maintaining inventory. The EOQ model uses mathematical formulas to calculate the ideal order quantity by balancing these two cost components. By ordering the precise quantity that minimizes the combined costs, businesses can achieve significant cost savings and operational efficiency. The EOQ formula considers factors such as demand rate, ordering costs, and holding costs, providing a systematic approach to inventory management. Implementing EOQ helps organizations reduce excess inventory, avoid stockouts, and improve cash flow by ensuring that resources are used efficiently. This optimization strategy is particularly valuable for businesses with consistent demand patterns, enabling them to maintain optimal inventory levels while minimizing costs.

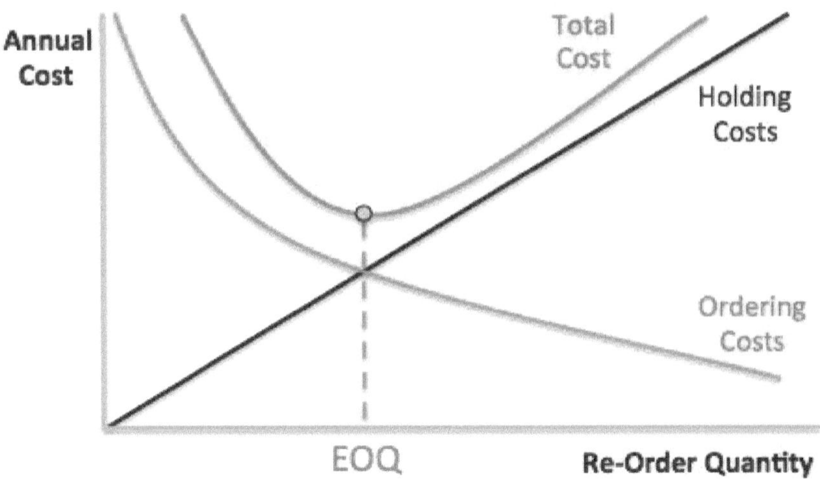

Economic Order Quantity (EOQ)

$$EOQ = \sqrt{\frac{2 * Demand * Ordering\ Costs}{Holding\ Costs}}$$

Formula

8. **Cycle Counting:** Cycle counting is an efficient inventory management technique that involves regularly counting a subset of inventory items to maintain accuracy in inventory records and identify discrepancies. Unlike traditional full-scale physical inventory audits, cycle counting is a continuous process where inventory is periodically checked throughout the year. This method focuses on counting small, manageable portions of the inventory, typically categorized by their value or importance using techniques like ABC analysis. By conducting frequent and systematic counts, businesses can promptly detect and correct discrepancies, such as missing or misplaced items, inaccuracies in records, and potential theft. Cycle counting helps maintain high levels of inventory accuracy, which is crucial for effective inventory control, demand forecasting, and customer satisfaction. Moreover, it minimizes operational disruptions since it can be integrated into daily workflows without requiring a complete halt in operations. Overall, cycle counting enhances inventory management by providing real-time data, reducing errors, and improving overall efficiency in inventory processes.

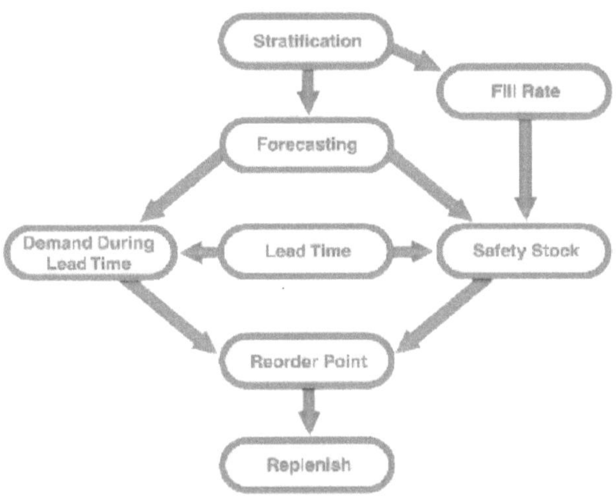

Inventory Management

By implementing these practices, organizations can optimize their inventory levels, reduce costs, and improve customer satisfaction. Advanced technologies, such as artificial intelligence and machine learning, are also being increasingly used to enhance inventory management processes, providing real-time insights and predictive analytics to support decision-making. Ultimately, effective inventory management is crucial for maintaining a balanced supply chain and achieving operational excellence.

CHAPTER NINE

PRODUCTION SCHEDULING

Production scheduling is a crucial process in industrial engineering that involves meticulously planning and organizing production activities to ensure goods are produced efficiently, on time, and within budget. The primary objective is to achieve a harmonious balance among various factors such as demand, production capacity, available resources, and time constraints. By developing an optimal production plan, production scheduling minimizes downtime, reduces bottlenecks, and ensures that resources are utilized effectively. This process involves coordinating the timing and sequence of tasks, allocating labor and equipment, and managing the flow of materials through the production system. Advanced scheduling techniques, such as Gantt charts, Critical Path Method (CPM), and software-based scheduling tools, help visualize and optimize the production process. By effectively managing these elements, production scheduling ensures that products are delivered to customers in a timely manner, maintaining high levels of customer satisfaction and competitiveness. Additionally, it allows organizations to respond swiftly to changes in demand and production requirements, enhancing overall operational agility and efficiency.

Here are key aspects of production scheduling:

1. **Demand Forecasting:** Demand forecasting is an essential aspect of supply chain and production management, involving the use of historical data and market analysis to predict future demand and plan production accordingly. By analyzing past sales trends, customer behavior, and external market factors, businesses can generate accurate demand

forecasts that guide production planning and inventory management. These forecasts help organizations anticipate fluctuations in demand, enabling them to adjust their production schedules and inventory levels to meet customer needs effectively. Advanced statistical methods and machine learning algorithms enhance the accuracy of demand forecasting by identifying patterns and correlations in large datasets. Additionally, market analysis considers factors such as economic conditions, seasonal trends, and competitor activities to provide a comprehensive understanding of future demand. By leveraging demand forecasting, companies can optimize resource allocation, reduce the risk of stockouts or overstock situations, and improve overall operational efficiency. Ultimately, effective demand forecasting supports better decision-making, enhances customer satisfaction, and contributes to the long-term success of the organization.

2. **Resource Allocation:** Resource allocation is a critical process in industrial engineering that involves strategically assigning resources such as labor, machinery, and materials to various production tasks to maximize efficiency and minimize downtime. Effective resource allocation ensures that the right resources are available at the right time and place, enabling seamless production operations. This process begins with a thorough analysis of production requirements, including the volume of work, the complexity of tasks, and the availability of resources. By optimizing the use of labor, machinery, and materials, organizations can avoid bottlenecks, reduce idle time, and enhance overall productivity. Advanced planning and scheduling tools, such as Enterprise Resource Planning (ERP) systems and optimization algorithms, play a vital role in resource allocation by providing real-time data and insights for informed decision-making. Additionally, considering factors such as worker skills, machine capabilities, and material quality ensures that resources are utilized to their fullest potential. Overall, effective resource allocation leads to improved operational efficiency, cost savings, and timely delivery of products, contributing to the success and competitiveness of the organization.
3. **Capacity Planning:** Capacity planning is a vital process in industrial engineering that ensures production facilities have the necessary capacity to meet demand efficiently and effectively. This involves evaluating and adjusting various elements such as work schedules, machine utilization, and workforce levels to match the production

requirements. By analyzing historical data and forecasting future demand, businesses can identify potential capacity constraints and develop strategies to address them. This may include adjusting work shifts, optimizing machine usage to minimize downtime, and reallocating or hiring additional workforce as needed. Effective capacity planning helps prevent production bottlenecks, reduces lead times, and ensures that resources are used to their full potential. Advanced tools and techniques, such as capacity requirement planning (CRP) and finite capacity scheduling (FCS), enable organizations to model different scenarios and make informed decisions. Ultimately, capacity planning enhances operational efficiency, improves customer satisfaction by meeting delivery deadlines, and supports the organization's ability to respond flexibly to changes in demand.

4. **Prioritization and Sequencing:** Prioritization and sequencing are essential components of production scheduling, focusing on determining the optimal order in which tasks should be performed to achieve production goals efficiently. This involves evaluating various factors such as due dates, production objectives, and resource availability to create a well-organized and effective production plan. By prioritizing tasks based on their urgency and importance, businesses can ensure that critical deadlines are met and customer demands are satisfied. Sequencing tasks involves arranging them in a logical and efficient order, taking into account dependencies and the availability of resources such as labor, machinery, and materials. Advanced scheduling techniques, such as Gantt charts and Critical Path Method (CPM), help visualize the sequence of tasks and identify potential bottlenecks. Effective prioritization and sequencing minimize downtime, optimize resource utilization, and enhance overall production efficiency. By strategically managing the order of tasks, organizations can achieve a smooth and continuous workflow, leading to timely delivery of products and improved operational performance.
5. **Scheduling Methods:** Scheduling methods are essential tools in industrial engineering that facilitate the creation and management of efficient production schedules. Techniques such as Gantt charts, Critical Path Method (CPM), and Enterprise Resource Planning (ERP) systems play a pivotal role in organizing and optimizing production activities.

   Gantt charts are visual representations that illustrate the timeline of tasks and their dependencies, providing a clear overview of the project schedule. They help identify task sequences, allocate resources, and monitor progress, ensuring that production stays on track.

Critical Path Method (CPM) is a project management technique that identifies the longest sequence of dependent tasks, known as the critical path, which determines the project's minimum completion time. By focusing on the critical path, organizations can prioritize tasks that directly impact the overall schedule, manage potential delays, and allocate resources effectively to ensure timely project completion.

Enterprise Resource Planning (ERP) systems integrate various business processes, including production scheduling, into a single unified platform. ERP systems provide real-time data and insights, enabling organizations to create dynamic and responsive schedules. They facilitate seamless communication and coordination across departments, optimize resource allocation, and enhance decision-making.

By implementing these scheduling methods, businesses can streamline production processes, improve resource utilization, and ensure that products are delivered on time and within budget. These techniques collectively contribute to higher operational efficiency, better project management, and increased customer satisfaction.

6. **Real-Time Monitoring:** Continuously tracking production progress and making adjustments as needed to address any issues or delays.

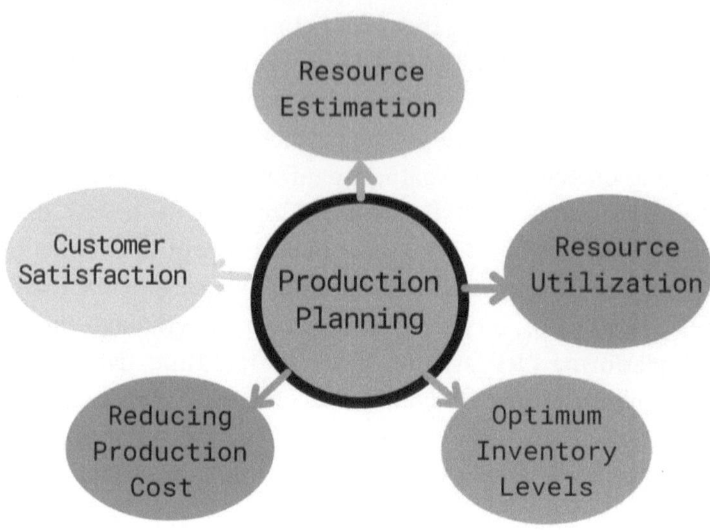

Production Scheduling

Effective production scheduling helps organizations improve productivity, reduce lead times, minimize costs, and enhance overall operational efficiency. By optimizing the production process, companies can better meet customer demands, maintain high-quality standards, and remain competitive in the market.

CHAPTER TEN

Total Quality Management (TQM)

Total Quality Management (TQM) is a comprehensive and holistic management approach that seeks to continuously enhance the quality of products and services by involving all employees and integrating quality-related activities into every facet of an organization. TQM emphasizes the importance of a customer-focused philosophy, where the ultimate aim is to exceed customer expectations and ensure their satisfaction. This involves adopting a proactive stance on quality, with every employee, from top management to frontline workers, participating in quality improvement initiatives. The TQM approach promotes a culture of continuous improvement, encouraging regular assessment and refinement of processes, products, and services to achieve higher standards of performance.

Key principles of TQM include leadership commitment, employee empowerment, and a strong focus on process management. Leadership plays a critical role in fostering a quality-centric culture, providing direction, support, and resources to achieve quality objectives. Employee empowerment involves training and encouraging employees to take ownership of quality in their respective roles, contributing to problem-solving and innovation. Process management entails a systematic approach to identifying, analyzing, and improving processes to eliminate inefficiencies and enhance quality.

By integrating these principles, TQM aims to increase efficiency, reduce waste, and optimize resource utilization, ultimately leading to higher productivity and cost savings. Through continuous feedback loops, performance metrics, and rigorous quality controls, TQM ensures that quality improvements are sustained and that the organization remains agile and responsive to changing customer needs and market conditions. In essence, TQM fosters a culture of excellence, where quality is ingrained in every aspect of the organization's operations, driving long-term success and competitiveness.

Key principles of TQM include:

1. **Customer Focus:** Customer focus is a cornerstone of Total Quality Management (TQM) and involves a deep commitment to understanding and meeting the needs and expectations of customers. This principle emphasizes that the ultimate measure of quality is customer satisfaction. To achieve this, organizations adopt a proactive approach to collecting and analyzing customer feedback through various channels, such as surveys, focus groups, social media interactions, and direct communications. This feedback provides invaluable insights into customer preferences, pain points, and expectations, enabling the organization to identify areas for improvement.

   By systematically gathering and utilizing customer feedback, businesses can drive continuous improvement initiatives that enhance product and service quality. This process involves identifying customer requirements, translating them into specific quality standards, and ensuring that all aspects of the organization's operations align with these standards. Additionally, fostering strong customer relationships and maintaining open lines of communication are essential for building trust and loyalty.

   A customer-focused approach ensures that the organization remains agile and responsive to changing market demands, ultimately leading to increased customer satisfaction and loyalty. This focus on the customer permeates every level of the organization, encouraging a culture of quality and excellence where every employee is dedicated to delivering superior value to the customer. By prioritizing customer needs and continuously striving to exceed their expectations, TQM helps organizations achieve long-term success and a competitive advantage in the marketplace.
2. **Employee Involvement:** Employee involvement is a fundamental principle of Total Quality Management (TQM), emphasizing that every individual within an organization, from top management to frontline workers, plays a vital role in maintaining and improving quality. Encouraging employees to take ownership of quality involves several key

strategies:

Training and DevelopmentProviding comprehensive training programs that equip employees with the necessary skills and knowledge to identify and address quality issues. This includes training in quality management principles, problem-solving techniques, and continuous improvement methodologies.

Empowerment Granting employees the authority and responsibility to make decisions related to quality within their areas of expertise. Empowered employees are more likely to take initiative, suggest improvements, and take proactive steps to prevent quality issues.

Collaborative Work EnvironmentFostering a culture of collaboration and open communication where employees feel valued and encouraged to share their ideas and feedback. Creating cross-functional teams and encouraging teamwork can enhance the collective problem-solving capabilities of the organization.

Recognition and IncentivesAcknowledging and rewarding employees' contributions to quality improvement can motivate and reinforce their commitment to maintaining high standards. Recognition programs, performance incentives, and opportunities for career advancement can drive continuous engagement in quality initiatives.

Feedback MechanismsEstablishing robust feedback systems that allow employees to voice their concerns, report issues, and provide suggestions for improvement. Regular feedback loops ensure that employees' insights are taken into consideration and acted upon.

By integrating these strategies, organizations can cultivate a strong sense of ownership and accountability among employees, leading to a more committed and motivated workforce. This, in turn, drives continuous improvement, enhances overall quality, and contributes to the long-term success and competitiveness of the organization.

3. **Process-Centric Approach:** A process-centric approach is a cornerstone of Total Quality Management (TQM), highlighting the critical role of managing and improving processes to achieve consistent and predictable results. This method begins with mapping out processes in detail, creating a clear visualization of each step involved in the production or service delivery. By thoroughly understanding the workflow, organizations can identify inefficiencies, bottlenecks, and areas that need improvement.

Once processes are mapped, the next step is to analyze and pinpoint specific areas where enhancements can be made. This may involve adopting new technologies, streamlining steps, or eliminating redundant tasks to optimize the process. Implementing standardized procedures is essential to maintain consistency and ensure that best practices are followed across the organization. Standardization helps in reducing variability and ensures that all employees perform tasks in a uniform manner, which leads to predictable and high-quality outcomes.

In addition to standardization, continuous monitoring and evaluation are vital to a process-centric approach. This involves regularly reviewing processes to assess their effectiveness and making necessary adjustments to adapt to changing conditions or new insights. Tools such as process audits, statistical process control (SPC), and Six Sigma methodologies can be employed to systematically improve process performance.

Overall, a process-centric approach fosters a culture of continuous improvement, where every aspect of the organization is geared towards achieving excellence. By focusing on processes, organizations can enhance efficiency, reduce costs, and deliver superior quality products and services that consistently meet or exceed customer expectations.

4. **Integrated System:** An integrated system in Total Quality Management (TQM) ensures that quality management principles are woven into every function and department of an organization, creating a cohesive and unified approach. This integration aligns quality initiatives with the overall business goals and objectives, fostering a culture where quality is a shared responsibility across the entire organization.

   In an integrated system, each department, whether it's production, sales, marketing, or human resources, works collaboratively towards common quality standards and objectives. This holistic approach ensures that quality management is not confined to a single department but is an organization-wide commitment. By embedding quality processes into everyday operations, organizations can streamline workflows, enhance communication, and improve overall efficiency.

   The integration also involves establishing standardized procedures, performance metrics, and continuous improvement practices that are consistently applied across all functions. This ensures that everyone in the organization is working towards the same quality goals and adhering to the same standards. Regular cross-functional meetings, training sessions, and quality audits help maintain alignment and foster a culture of continuous improvement.

Ultimately, an integrated system enhances organizational coherence, reduces silos, and drives synergy, leading to improved performance, higher customer satisfaction, and long-term success. By aligning quality management with business objectives, organizations can achieve a seamless and efficient operation that consistently delivers high-quality products and services.

5. **Strategic and Systematic Approach:** A strategic and systematic approach is fundamental to the successful implementation of Total Quality Management (TQM). This approach ensures that quality improvement initiatives are not conducted in isolation but are deeply aligned with the organization's overarching mission, vision, and long-term goals. It begins with the development of a strategic plan that clearly defines quality objectives and the steps needed to achieve them.

   Setting quality objectives involves identifying specific, measurable, achievable, relevant, and time-bound (SMART) goals that reflect the organization's commitment to quality. These objectives should be integrated into the broader business strategy, ensuring that quality improvement is a central focus across all functions and departments.

   To translate these objectives into actionable plans, organizations must develop detailed action plans that outline the tasks, responsibilities, resources, and timelines required to achieve the desired quality outcomes. This involves coordinating efforts across different teams and departments, fostering collaboration, and ensuring that everyone is aligned towards common quality goals.

   Additionally, a strategic and systematic approach includes regular monitoring and evaluation of progress towards quality objectives. This involves using key performance indicators (KPIs) and other metrics to assess the effectiveness of quality initiatives and making necessary adjustments to stay on track. By maintaining a clear focus on long-term goals and continuously aligning quality efforts with the organization's mission and vision, businesses can drive sustained improvements, enhance customer satisfaction, and achieve a competitive advantage in the marketplace.

6. **Continuous Improvement:** Continuous improvement, often referred to by the Japanese term "Kaizen," is a fundamental principle of Total Quality Management (TQM) that promotes ongoing, incremental

enhancements to processes, products, and services. This philosophy is rooted in the belief that even small, continuous changes can lead to significant long-term improvements and contribute to the overall success of the organization.

The practice of continuous improvement involves a systematic approach where employees at all levels are encouraged to identify opportunities for improvement and implement solutions. This process typically includes regular review and analysis of current workflows, identifying inefficiencies, and brainstorming potential enhancements. By fostering a culture of continuous improvement, organizations create an environment where innovation and proactive problem-solving are integral parts of everyday operations.

Key elements of Kaizen include:

Employee Empowerment Involving employees in the decision-making process and encouraging them to take ownership of quality improvements. This ensures that those closest to the processes are actively contributing to enhancements.

Standardization Implementing standardized procedures that can be consistently applied across the organization, ensuring that improvements are maintained and replicated.

Feedback Loops Establishing mechanisms for regular feedback and evaluation, allowing for continuous monitoring and refinement of processes.

Cross-Functional Teams Creating teams that span various departments to collaborate on improvement initiatives, bringing diverse perspectives and expertise to the table.

By adhering to the principles of continuous improvement, organizations can achieve greater efficiency, reduce waste, and enhance the quality of their offerings. This not only leads to higher customer satisfaction but also strengthens the organization's ability to adapt to changing market conditions and maintain a competitive edge. Ultimately, the Kaizen approach drives long-term, sustainable success by embedding a culture of excellence and perpetual growth.

7. **Fact-Based Decision Making:** Fact-based decision making is a core principle of Total Quality Management (TQM) that emphasizes the importance of using data and analysis to guide decisions related to quality improvement, rather than relying on intuition or guesswork. This approach ensures that decisions are objective, reliable, and aligned with

the organization's goals for continuous improvement.

To implement fact-based decision making, organizations need to collect relevant data from various sources, such as production records, customer feedback, process measurements, and financial reports. This data provides valuable insights into the performance of processes, products, and services. By analyzing this data, organizations can identify trends, patterns, and areas of improvement that may not be immediately apparent.

Advanced data analysis techniques, such as statistical process control (SPC), Six Sigma methodologies, and data mining, can be used to uncover root causes of quality issues and assess the effectiveness of improvement initiatives. Key performance indicators (KPIs) and other metrics are established to measure progress and ensure that the organization is on track to achieve its quality objectives.

By making decisions based on empirical evidence, organizations can minimize risks, reduce variability, and enhance the predictability of outcomes. This leads to more informed and effective decision-making, ultimately resulting in improved quality, higher efficiency, and greater customer satisfaction. Fact-based decision making fosters a culture of accountability and transparency, where every decision is backed by data and aligned with the organization's commitment to excellence.

8. **Communication:** Effective communication is a cornerstone of Total Quality Management (TQM), ensuring that everyone within the organization comprehends their roles in the quality improvement process and is aligned with the overarching goals. Clear and open communication channels are vital at all levels, facilitating the seamless flow of information across departments and hierarchies. This includes regular meetings, training sessions, and updates where employees can discuss quality-related issues, share insights, and collaborate on solutions. Transparent communication fosters a culture of trust and accountability, encouraging employees to voice their ideas and concerns freely. Additionally, effective communication involves providing timely feedback, recognizing achievements, and addressing any challenges promptly. By maintaining open lines of communication, organizations can ensure that all members are informed, engaged, and committed to continuous improvement, ultimately leading to enhanced quality, customer satisfaction, and organizational success.

Total Quality Management (TQM)

Implementing TQM can lead to numerous benefits, such as higher customer satisfaction, reduced costs, improved efficiency, and enhanced employee morale. By embedding quality into every aspect of the organization, TQM helps create a culture of excellence that drives long-term success and competitiveness.

CHAPTER ELEVEN

Six Sigma and Lean Manufacturing

Six Sigma and Lean Manufacturing are two complementary methodologies aimed at improving efficiency, quality, and productivity in industrial processes. Six Sigma focuses on reducing process variability and eliminating defects through a data-driven approach, using tools like DMAIC (Define, Measure, Analyze, Improve, Control) to achieve near-perfect quality standards. On the other hand, Lean Manufacturing emphasizes minimizing waste and optimizing workflows by streamlining processes, reducing redundancies, and maximizing value for customers. Together, these approaches enhance operational performance, reduce costs, and improve customer satisfaction by fostering a culture of continuous improvement and precision in manufacturing and other business processes.

Six Sigma and Lean Manufacturing are two powerful methodologies in industrial engineering that focus on improving processes, enhancing efficiency, and reducing waste.

Six Sigma

Six Sigma is a data-driven approach that focuses on reducing process variation and eliminating defects to achieve near-perfect quality. It employs a structured methodology known as DMAIC (Define, Measure, Analyze, Improve, Control) to systematically identify and eliminate sources of errors and inefficiencies. By using statistical tools and techniques, Six Sigma practitioners can analyze processes in detail, pinpoint root causes of defects, and implement solutions that lead to significant quality improvements. The ultimate goal is to achieve a Six Sigma level of quality, which corresponds to a defect rate of 3.4 per million opportunities, thus ensuring high reliability and customer satisfaction.

The Six Sigma approach is structured around the DMAIC framework: The DMAIC methodology, central to Six Sigma, is a structured problem-solving process comprising five key phases: Define, Measure, Analyze, Improve, and Control.

1. **Define:** The first phase involves clearly identifying the problem, establishing the project goals, and understanding the customer requirements. This includes defining the scope of the project, setting objectives, and determining the critical quality aspects that impact customer satisfaction. By clearly outlining the problem and goals, the team sets a solid foundation for the improvement project.
2. **Measure:** In this phase, relevant data is collected to establish a baseline of the current process performance. This involves identifying key performance indicators (KPIs), gathering data on process outputs, and measuring the existing level of defects or variability. Accurate measurement is crucial to understand the current state and to quantify the extent of the problem.
3. **Analyze:** The analysis phase focuses on examining the collected data to identify the root causes of defects and variability within the process. Statistical tools and techniques are used to uncover patterns, correlations, and underlying factors contributing to the problem. This phase aims to pinpoint the critical sources of inefficiencies and areas that need improvement.
4. **Improve:** Based on the insights gained from the analysis phase, solutions are developed and implemented to eliminate the identified root causes and enhance the process. This may involve redesigning workflows, adopting new technologies, or introducing process changes. The goal is to make targeted improvements that lead to measurable enhancements in performance.
5. **Control:** The final phase involves establishing control measures to sustain the improvements and ensure consistent performance over time. This includes implementing monitoring systems, standardizing procedures, and setting up regular audits to track progress. Control measures help maintain the gains achieved and prevent the recurrence of issues, ensuring long-term success.

By following the DMAIC methodology, organizations can systematically improve their processes, reduce defects, and achieve higher levels of quality and efficiency. This structured approach provides a clear roadmap for continuous improvement, driving better business outcomes and enhanced customer satisfaction.

Lean Manufacturing

Lean Manufacturing, on the other hand, emphasizes the elimination of waste (or "muda") in all forms, including excess inventory, overproduction, waiting times, unnecessary transportation, inefficient processes, defects, and underutilized talent. Lean principles advocate for creating more value with fewer resources by streamlining workflows, optimizing resource utilization, and fostering a culture of continuous improvement. Key Lean tools and concepts include Value Stream Mapping, 5S (Sort, Set in order, Shine, Standardize, Sustain), Kaizen (continuous improvement), and Just-In-Time (JIT) production. By focusing on maximizing value and minimizing waste, Lean Manufacturing helps organizations improve efficiency, reduce costs, and enhance overall operational performance.

Key principles of Lean Manufacturing include: Lean Manufacturing is built on key principles that drive efficiency and minimize waste, ultimately enhancing overall value delivery. These principles include:

1. **Value:** The cornerstone of Lean Manufacturing is identifying what the customer truly values and focusing efforts on delivering that value. By understanding customer needs and preferences, organizations can tailor their processes to create products and services that meet or exceed customer expectations, enhancing satisfaction and loyalty.
2. **Value Stream:** Mapping out the entire value stream involves visualizing and analyzing every step in the production process, from raw material to finished product. This comprehensive view helps identify and eliminate non-value-added activities or waste, such as excess inventory, waiting times, and unnecessary movements. Streamlining the value stream enhances efficiency and reduces costs.
3. **Flow:** Ensuring a smooth flow of materials and information through the value stream is critical to maintaining efficiency. This involves organizing processes and workspaces to minimize interruptions, delays, and bottlenecks. By creating a continuous flow, organizations can reduce lead times, improve responsiveness, and increase overall productivity.
4. **Pull:** Implementing a pull system means producing only what is needed when it is needed, based on actual customer demand rather than forecasted demand. This approach reduces overproduction, excess

inventory, and associated carrying costs. Pull systems, such as Just-In-Time (JIT) production, ensure that resources are used efficiently and waste is minimized.

5. **Perfection:** The pursuit of perfection is a fundamental principle of Lean Manufacturing, emphasizing continuous improvement (Kaizen) in every aspect of the process. Organizations are encouraged to regularly assess and refine their processes, products, and services to achieve higher standards of quality and efficiency. This commitment to ongoing improvement drives innovation and long-term success.

Integration of Six Sigma and Lean

When combined, Six Sigma and Lean methodologies create a powerful approach known as Lean Six Sigma. This hybrid methodology leverages the strengths of both approaches: the statistical rigor and focus on quality from Six Sigma, and the waste reduction and efficiency focus from Lean. By integrating these methodologies, organizations can achieve higher levels of performance, quality, and customer satisfaction.

In practice, Lean Six Sigma projects often start with Lean principles to streamline processes and eliminate waste, followed by Six Sigma tools to reduce variability and improve quality. This integrated approach ensures a comprehensive and systematic improvement strategy that drives continuous growth and operational excellence.

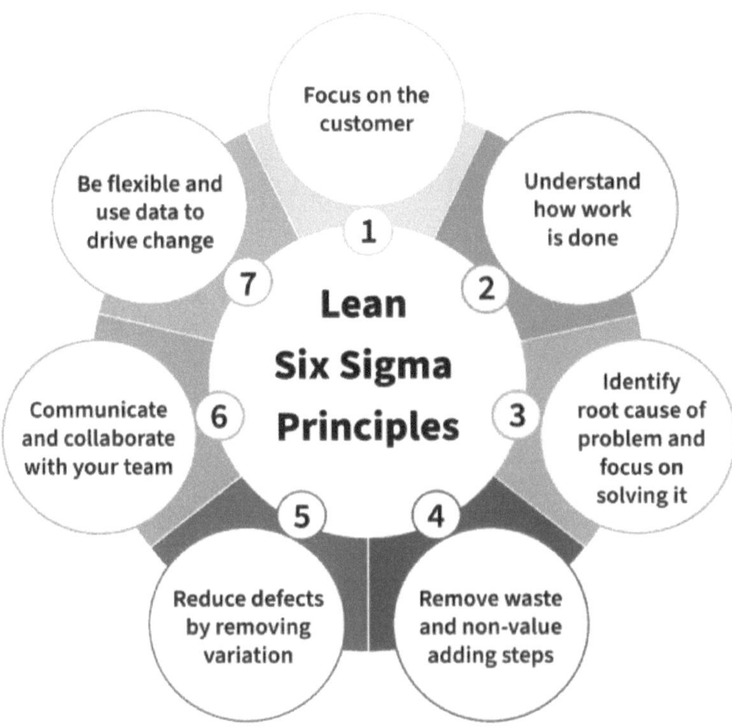

Lean Six Sigma Principles

By adhering to these principles, Lean Manufacturing enables organizations to create more value with fewer resources, achieve higher levels of efficiency, and maintain a competitive edge in the marketplace.

CHAPTER TWELVE

LINEAR PROGRAMMING

Linear programming is a powerful mathematical optimization technique extensively utilized in industrial engineering to determine the most optimal outcome within a given mathematical model. This technique entails formulating a problem with a linear objective function and a set of linear constraints. The primary aim is to either maximize or minimize the objective function, which could represent various goals such as profit, cost, production output, or resource allocation.

Linear programming is a mathematical optimization technique used to determine the best possible outcome in a given model, subject to certain constraints. It involves representing a problem using linear equations and inequalities, where an objective function, typically aimed at minimizing costs or maximizing profits, is optimized within the defined constraints. Widely applied in industries such as manufacturing, logistics, and resource allocation, linear programming helps in solving complex problems like determining the optimal production schedule, minimizing transportation costs, or efficiently utilizing resources. Its systematic approach enables decision-makers to achieve optimal results while adhering to limitations, making it a valuable tool in operational planning and management.

The process begins with defining the objective function, which quantitatively expresses the goal to be achieved. This function is then subject to a series of linear constraints, which represent the limitations or requirements of the problem, such as resource availability, production capacity, or demand constraints. These constraints are expressed as linear equations or inequalities.

By solving the linear programming model, organizations can identify the best possible solution that satisfies all constraints while optimizing the objective function. This optimal solution provides valuable insights into resource allocation, production planning, and decision-making, enabling businesses to achieve their goals efficiently.

Linear programming techniques, such as the Simplex method or interior-point methods, are used to solve these models, providing precise and actionable solutions. The versatility and effectiveness of linear programming make it an essential tool in industrial engineering, driving improvements in operational efficiency, cost reduction, and overall performance.

Key Concepts in Linear Programming

1. **Objective Function:** The objective function in linear programming is a linear equation that quantitatively represents the goal of the optimization problem. This function serves as the criterion that needs to be maximized or minimized, depending on the specific objective of the problem. Common goals include maximizing profit, minimizing costs, maximizing production output, or optimizing resource utilization. The objective function is formulated based on the variables and coefficients that represent the various elements influencing the outcome. For example, in a profit maximization problem, the objective function may include variables representing different products, with their respective profit margins as coefficients. By optimizing the objective function, organizations can determine the best possible solution that achieves the desired outcome while satisfying all the given constraints. This process enables efficient decision-making and resource allocation, ultimately leading to improved operational performance and goal attainment.
2. **Decision Variables:** Decision variables are the critical unknowns in a linear programming problem that need to be determined in order to achieve the optimal solution. These variables represent the quantities or levels of different activities, resources, or products that the organization can control and adjust. In the context of linear programming, decision variables are typically denoted by symbols such as x1,x2,x3,x_1, x_2, x_3, and so on.

   The values of these decision variables are what we seek to determine through the optimization process. For example, in a production planning problem, decision variables might represent the number of units of each product to be produced. In a resource allocation problem, they could represent the amount of resources to be allocated to different tasks or projects.

By defining and solving for these decision variables, we can determine the best possible combination that maximizes or minimizes the objective function, while satisfying all the given constraints. The optimal values of the decision variables provide actionable insights for decision-making, enabling organizations to achieve their goals efficiently and effectively. Ultimately, decision variables are the key levers that drive the optimization process, leading to improved performance and outcomes.

3. **Constraints:** Constraints are essential components of a linear programming problem, representing the limitations or requirements that must be considered when seeking an optimal solution. These constraints are expressed as linear inequalities or equations and define the boundaries within which the decision variables can operate. Common types of constraints include resource availability, production capacity, budget limitations, and demand requirements.

   For instance, in a production planning problem, constraints might specify the maximum number of hours available for labor, the capacity of machinery, or the availability of raw materials. These constraints ensure that the solution remains feasible and practical, adhering to real-world limitations. For example, a constraint could be expressed as 2x1+3x2≤1002x_1 + 3x_2 \leq 100, where x1x_1 and x2x_2 are decision variables representing the quantities of two products, and 100 represents the maximum production capacity.

   By incorporating constraints into the linear programming model, organizations can ensure that the optimal solution not only maximizes or minimizes the objective function but also respects the specified limitations. This approach provides a realistic and actionable solution that can be implemented effectively within the given constraints, leading to improved decision-making and operational efficiency. Constraints play a crucial role in guiding the optimization process, ensuring that the results align with the organization's goals and available resources.

4. **Feasible Region:** The feasible region in linear programming is a crucial concept representing the set of all possible solutions that satisfy the given constraints. This region is typically depicted as a geometric area on a graph, where each point within this area corresponds to a combination

of decision variable values that meet all the specified limitations, such as resource availability, production capacity, and other requirements. The feasible region is bounded by the constraints, which are expressed as linear inequalities or equations. The optimal solution to the linear programming problem must lie within this region, as it represents the most favorable outcome that adheres to all constraints. By identifying the feasible region, organizations can visualize the range of potential solutions and focus their efforts on finding the best possible solution that maximizes or minimizes the objective function while remaining within the acceptable boundaries defined by the constraints. This approach ensures that the solution is both practical and achievable, leading to improved decision-making and operational efficiency.

Formulating a Linear Programming Problem

Formulating a linear programming problem involves several key steps that translate a real-world scenario into a mathematical model, enabling the determination of an optimal solution. The process begins by clearly defining the objective of the problem, whether it is to maximize or minimize a particular quantity, such as profit, cost, or resource utilization. This objective is expressed as a linear objective function, which quantifies the goal in terms of decision variables.

Next, decision variables are identified, representing the unknown quantities that need to be determined to achieve the optimal solution. These variables are the key factors that can be controlled and adjusted within the problem.

Once the decision variables are established, the constraints of the problem are formulated. Constraints are linear inequalities or equations that represent the limitations or requirements of the problem, such as resource availability, production capacity, budget limits, or demand fulfillment. These constraints define the feasible region, which is the set of all possible solutions that satisfy the constraints.

The formulation process also involves ensuring that the objective function and constraints are linear, meaning they involve no more than first-degree terms of the decision variables.

- To summarize, formulating a linear programming problem involves:
- Defining the objective function to be maximized or minimized.
- Identifying the decision variables that need to be determined.

- Establishing the linear constraints that represent the problem's limitations or requirements.

By following these steps, a clear and structured mathematical model is created, allowing for the application of linear programming techniques to find the optimal solution within the feasible region. This systematic approach facilitates informed decision-making and efficient resource allocation, leading to improved outcomes and operational performance.

To formulate a linear programming problem, follow these steps:

1. **Define the Decision Variables:** Defining decision variables is a crucial step in formulating a linear programming problem, as these variables represent the unknowns that need to be determined to achieve the optimal solution. Decision variables are the controllable factors that influence the outcome of the objective function and are subject to the given constraints.

   When identifying decision variables, it is essential to ensure that they accurately represent the key elements of the problem. For instance, in a production planning scenario, decision variables might include the number of units of each product to be produced. In a resource allocation problem, they could represent the amount of resources allocated to different tasks or projects.

   Each decision variable should be clearly defined with a specific symbol or notation (e.g., x1,x2,x3x_1, x_2, x_3) and should have a meaningful interpretation within the context of the problem. The definition of decision variables sets the foundation for formulating the objective function and constraints, as these variables will be used to express the relationships and interactions within the problem.

   By accurately defining the decision variables, organizations can ensure that the linear programming model effectively captures the essence of the problem, leading to a more precise and actionable optimal solution. This step is fundamental to the success of the optimization process, enabling informed decision-making and efficient resource allocation.
2. **Construct the Objective Function:** Constructing the objective function is a pivotal step in formulating a linear programming problem, as it defines the goal of the optimization in the form of a linear equation. The objective function quantitatively expresses the target that needs to be

achieved, whether it is to maximize or minimize a particular metric such as profit, cost, production output, or resource utilization.

To create the objective function, the decision variables identified earlier are used in combination with their corresponding coefficients. These coefficients represent the contribution of each decision variable to the overall objective. For example, in a profit maximization problem, the coefficients would be the profit margins associated with each product, while the decision variables would represent the quantities of each product to be produced.

The objective function is typically expressed in the following form:

$$Z = c_1x_1 + c_2x_2 + c_3x_3 + \ ... \ + c_nx_n$$

where:

- Z is the value of the objective function to be maximized or minimized.
- $c_1, c_2, c_3, \ldots, c_n$ are the coefficients representing the contribution of each decision variable to the objective.
- $x_1, x_2, x_3, \ldots, x_n$ are the decision variables.

For example, if a company aims to maximize profit by producing two products, A and B, with profit margins of $30 and $50 per unit respectively, and the decision variables x_1 and x_2 represent the quantities of products A and B to be produced, the objective function would be:

$$Z = 30x_1 + 50x_2$$

By constructing this linear equation, the objective function clearly specifies the goal of the optimization, providing a mathematical representation of what the organization seeks to achieve. This function, in conjunction with the constraints, forms the basis of the linear programming model, enabling the determination of the optimal solution that aligns with the defined goal.

3. **Establish the Constraints:** Establishing constraints is a vital step in formulating a linear programming problem, as these constraints define

the limitations or requirements that must be considered to find an optimal solution. Constraints are expressed as linear inequalities or equations that represent real-world restrictions such as resource availability, production capacity, budget limits, or demand requirements. These constraints ensure that the solution remains feasible and practical within the given boundaries. By establishing and formulating constraints, organizations can ensure that the linear programming model accurately reflects real-world limitations, leading to a feasible and actionable optimal solution. This structured approach enables efficient decision-making, resource allocation, and goal attainment, driving improved operational performance and outcomes.

4. **Identify the Feasible Region:** Identifying the feasible region is a critical step in solving a linear programming problem. The feasible region represents the set of all possible solutions that satisfy the given constraints. Determining this region involves graphically or analytically analyzing the constraints, which are typically expressed as linear inequalities or equations, to visualize the boundaries within which the decision variables must operate. The feasible region provides a visual and mathematical representation of all possible solutions to the linear programming problem. The optimal solution, which maximizes or minimizes the objective function, must lie within this region. By identifying the feasible region, organizations can focus their efforts on exploring solutions within the practical and realistic boundaries defined by the constraints, leading to effective and efficient decision-making.

Solution Methods

Several methods can be used to solve linear programming problems:

1. **Graphical Method:** The graphical method is a visual approach used for solving linear programming problems with two decision variables. This method involves plotting the constraints and the objective function on a graph to identify the feasible region and determine the optimal solution.

   The process begins by graphing each constraint as a line on a coordinate plane, with the decision variables represented on the x-axis and y-axis. The inequalities are then used to shade the areas that satisfy the constraints, revealing the feasible region where all constraints overlap. This region encompasses all possible solutions that meet the problem's requirements.

Next, the objective function is plotted as a line on the same graph. By moving this line parallel to itself, the goal is to find the point within the feasible region that either maximizes or minimizes the objective function, depending on the problem's goal. This point, often located at a vertex (or corner) of the feasible region, represents the optimal solution.

The graphical method provides a clear and intuitive way to visualize and solve linear programming problems, making it particularly useful for simpler problems with two decision variables. This approach helps in understanding the relationships between constraints and the objective function, leading to effective decision-making and optimal outcomes.

2. **Simplex Method:** The Simplex Method is an iterative algorithm widely used in linear programming to find the optimal solution for large-scale problems. This method systematically explores the edges of the feasible region, which is defined by the constraints of the problem, to identify the best possible outcome. The Simplex Method begins with an initial feasible solution, typically at a vertex (corner point) of the feasible region. From this starting point, the algorithm evaluates adjacent vertices along the edges of the region to determine which direction leads to an improvement in the objective function.

   At each iteration, the Simplex Method moves from the current vertex to an adjacent vertex that increases (or decreases) the value of the objective function, depending on whether the goal is to maximize or minimize it. This process continues until no further improvements can be made, indicating that the optimal solution has been reached. One of the key strengths of the Simplex Method is its ability to efficiently navigate the feasible region, even in problems with many constraints and decision variables.

   The Simplex Method's effectiveness and scalability make it a preferred choice for solving complex and large-scale linear programming problems in various fields, including industrial engineering, operations research, logistics, and finance. By providing precise and actionable solutions, the Simplex Method enables organizations to optimize resource allocation, enhance operational efficiency, and achieve their strategic objectives.

3. **Computer-Based Solutions:** Computer-based solutions are indispensable for efficiently solving complex linear programming problems, as they leverage powerful algorithms and computational capabilities to handle large-scale optimization tasks. Software tools such

as MATLAB, LINGO, and Excel Solver are among the most widely used applications for this purpose.

MATLAB: MATLAB is a high-performance computing environment that offers a range of tools for numerical computation, data analysis, and visualization. Its Optimization Toolbox provides functions for solving linear, nonlinear, and mixed-integer programming problems. MATLAB's intuitive interface and powerful computational capabilities make it an excellent choice for handling complex linear programming problems, enabling users to model, analyze, and solve optimization tasks with ease.

LINGO: LINGO is a specialized optimization software designed for solving linear, nonlinear, and integer programming problems. It offers a user-friendly modeling environment and a wide range of built-in solvers that can handle large-scale optimization tasks. LINGO's capabilities include automatic differentiation, sensitivity analysis, and integration with external data sources, making it a versatile and efficient tool for tackling complex linear programming challenges.

Excel Solver: Excel Solver is an add-in tool for Microsoft Excel that provides a straightforward and accessible way to solve linear programming problems. It allows users to define objective functions, decision variables, and constraints within the familiar Excel interface. Excel Solver is particularly useful for small to medium-sized problems and offers various solving methods, including Simplex and GRG Nonlinear algorithms. Its ease of use and integration with Excel make it a popular choice for business professionals and students alike.

By utilizing these computer-based solutions, organizations can efficiently solve complex linear programming problems, optimize resource allocation, and achieve their strategic objectives. These tools streamline the optimization process, provide accurate and actionable insights, and enhance decision-making capabilities, ultimately leading to improved operational performance and outcomes.

Applications of Linear Programming

Linear programming has a wide range of applications in industrial engineering, including:

- **Production Planning:** Production planning is a critical process in manufacturing and operations management that involves optimizing the allocation of resources to meet production targets while minimizing costs. This process ensures that the right amount of products is produced at the right time, using the most efficient combination of resources such as labor, materials, machinery, and equipment. The goal is to balance production capacity with customer demand, reduce waste, and improve overall operational efficiency.

- **Supply Chain Management:** Supply chain management is a critical aspect of operations that focuses on determining the optimal distribution of goods to minimize transportation costs while meeting customer demand. This involves the strategic coordination of various activities, including procurement, production, warehousing, and logistics, to ensure that products are delivered efficiently and effectively.
- **Inventory Control:** Inventory control is a vital aspect of operations management that involves managing inventory levels to balance holding costs and stockout risks effectively. The primary goal is to ensure that the right amount of inventory is available to meet customer demand without incurring excessive costs or facing shortages.

  Holding costs include expenses associated with storing and maintaining inventory, such as warehousing, insurance, depreciation, and opportunity costs of capital tied up in inventory. High holding costs can erode profitability, making it essential to keep inventory levels as low as possible while still meeting demand.

  Stockout risks, on the other hand, refer to the potential negative consequences of running out of inventory, such as lost sales, dissatisfied customers, and disruptions in production or service delivery. Stockouts can damage an organization's reputation and lead to long-term customer attrition.
- **Workforce Scheduling:** Workforce scheduling is a crucial aspect of operations management that involves assigning workers to shifts in a way that maximizes productivity and meets labor requirements. The primary objective is to ensure that the right number of employees with the appropriate skills are available at the right times to handle workload demands efficiently. Effective workforce scheduling takes into account several factors, including employee availability, labor laws and regulations, workload patterns, and operational needs.
- **Project Management:** Project management is an essential discipline that involves optimizing the allocation of resources and scheduling tasks to ensure projects are completed on time and within budget. The primary objective is to balance the competing constraints of scope, time, cost,

and quality to deliver successful project outcomes. Effective project management requires careful planning, coordination, and monitoring of various activities throughout the project lifecycle.

By applying linear programming techniques, industrial engineers can make informed decisions, optimize processes, and improve overall efficiency in various aspects of industrial operations.

CHAPTER THIRTEEN

SIMULATION AND MODELING

Simulation and modeling are indispensable tools in industrial engineering, enabling engineers to design, analyze, and optimize complex systems and processes. These techniques involve creating virtual representations of real-world systems, which can be used to predict and enhance performance under various conditions. By constructing detailed models that accurately reflect the behavior and interactions of system components, industrial engineers can conduct experiments, test scenarios, and evaluate the impact of different variables without disrupting actual operations. This approach allows for the identification of bottlenecks, inefficiencies, and potential improvements, leading to more informed decision-making and strategic planning. Simulation and modeling also facilitate risk assessment, enabling engineers to anticipate and mitigate potential issues before they occur. Ultimately, these tools contribute to greater operational efficiency, cost savings, and enhanced overall performance in industrial processes. Simulation and modeling are powerful tools used in industrial engineering and various other fields to analyze and optimize systems, processes, or products. Modeling involves creating a simplified representation of a real-world system, capturing its key components and interactions to understand its behavior. Simulation takes this a step further by using computational techniques to mimic the system's performance under different conditions and scenarios. These methods enable engineers to predict outcomes, identify inefficiencies, and test solutions without the cost and risk of real-world experimentation. Widely applied in areas such as manufacturing, logistics, and product design, simulation and modeling are essential for decision-making, improving efficiency, and fostering innovation while minimizing resource usage and environmental impact.

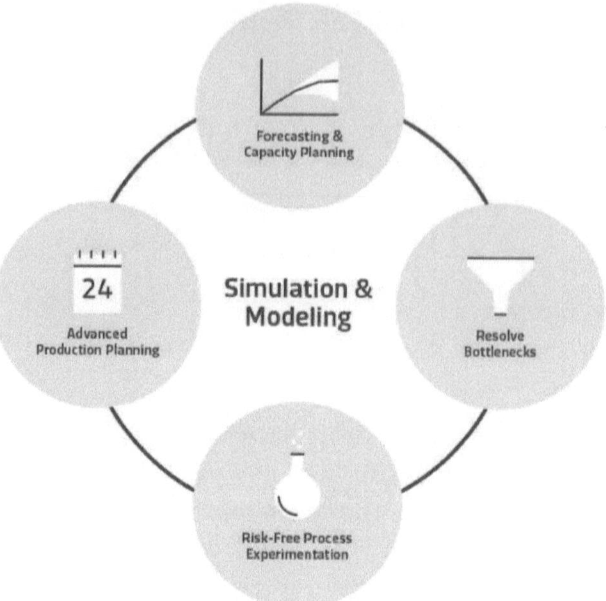

Simulation and Modeling

Concepts and Techniques
Modeling:

- **Conceptual Models:** Conceptual models are simplified representations of systems, capturing the essential features while deliberately omitting unnecessary details. These models serve as the foundation for more detailed analyses and provide a high-level understanding of the system's structure and behavior. By focusing on the key components and their relationships, conceptual models help engineers and decision-makers visualize complex processes and identify the most critical factors influencing system performance. These models are instrumental in the initial stages of system design and analysis, as they facilitate clear communication of ideas, hypotheses, and assumptions. Once a conceptual model is established, it can be refined and expanded into more detailed and quantitative models, enabling precise simulations and optimization of the system. Ultimately, conceptual models play a crucial role in guiding the development of effective solutions and strategies in industrial engineering.

- **Mathematical Models:** Mathematical models are analytical tools that use mathematical equations to describe the relationships between various components of a system. These models can range from simple linear equations, which involve straightforward, proportional relationships between variables, to complex non-linear systems, where interactions and dependencies are more intricate and can include feedback loops, exponential growth, and other non-linear behaviors.

  By representing systems mathematically, these models allow engineers and analysts to gain insights into how different factors influence system performance and behavior. For example, in a production process, a mathematical model might express the relationship between input resources (such as raw materials, labor, and machinery) and output products, taking into account constraints like production capacity and efficiency.

  Mathematical models are invaluable for simulation and optimization, as they enable precise calculations, predictions, and analysis of various scenarios. They can be used to identify optimal solutions, assess the impact of changes in system parameters, and explore potential improvements. These models provide a foundation for decision-making and strategic planning, helping organizations to optimize processes, reduce costs, and enhance overall performance.

  Overall, mathematical models serve as powerful tools for understanding and improving complex systems, offering a structured and quantitative approach to problem-solving in industrial engineering and beyond.

- **Computational Models:** Computational models leverage computer software to simulate the behavior of systems over time, providing a dynamic and detailed representation of complex processes. These models are particularly useful for analyzing systems that are too intricate for traditional analytical solutions, as they can account for numerous variables, interactions, and dependencies that would be challenging to capture otherwise.

  By using computational models, engineers and analysts can create virtual environments that mimic real-world systems, enabling them to observe how these systems evolve under various conditions and scenarios. This approach allows for the exploration of "what-if" scenarios, helping to predict outcomes and assess the impact of different factors on system performance.Computational models are widely used in various fields, including manufacturing, logistics, healthcare, finance, and environmental science. They provide a powerful tool for decision-making, allowing organizations to optimize processes, reduce risks, and enhance overall performance. By simulating complex systems in a virtual environment, computational models enable a deeper understanding of system dynamics and facilitate the development of effective solutions and strategies.

Simulation:

- **Discrete Event Simulation (DES):** Discrete Event Simulation (DES) is a powerful modeling technique that represents systems as a sequence of distinct events occurring at specific points in time. Each event triggers a change in the system's state, making DES particularly effective for analyzing and understanding complex processes where activities and interactions happen intermittently. By modeling these discrete events, DES provides a detailed and dynamic representation of the system's behavior over time.

  In DES, the system is represented by a series of events, each associated with specific actions or state changes. For example, in a manufacturing process, events might include the arrival of raw materials, the start and completion of production tasks, machine breakdowns, and the movement of finished products to storage. Each of these events causes the system to transition from one state to another, allowing for a granular analysis of how different factors impact overall performance.

  DES is widely used in various fields, including manufacturing and logistics, due to its ability to capture the intricacies of complex systems. In manufacturing, DES can model production lines, assembly processes, and supply chain operations, helping to identify bottlenecks, optimize resource utilization, and improve efficiency. In logistics, DES can simulate transportation networks, warehouse operations, and inventory management, enabling organizations to optimize routes, reduce costs, and enhance service levels.

  The strength of DES lies in its ability to model and analyze systems with variable and unpredictable behaviors. By simulating discrete events, engineers and analysts can experiment with different scenarios, test the impact of changes, and make informed decisions based on the simulation results. This approach provides valuable insights into system dynamics, facilitating continuous improvement and strategic planning.

Overall, Discrete Event Simulation is a versatile and effective tool for understanding and optimizing complex systems, making it an indispensable technique in industrial engineering and beyond.

- **System Dynamics (SD):** System Dynamics (SD) is a powerful modeling approach that focuses on understanding and predicting the behavior of complex systems over time. SD models utilize a combination of stocks, flows, feedback loops, and time delays to represent the intricate interactions within a system.

  Stocks represent the accumulations or quantities within the system, such as inventory levels, population, or capital. These stocks change over time as they are influenced by flows, which are the rates at which quantities enter or leave the stocks. For example, the inflow of raw materials into a warehouse and the outflow of finished products to customers.

  Feedback loops are fundamental to SD models, as they depict the cause-and-effect relationships that create dynamic behaviors. These loops can be reinforcing (positive feedback) or balancing (negative feedback), driving growth or stabilizing the system, respectively. For instance, a reinforcing loop might illustrate how increased production leads to higher sales and further increases in production, while a balancing loop might represent how rising inventory levels trigger reduced production rates.

  Time delays account for the lag between actions and their effects within the system. These delays are crucial for capturing the realistic temporal dynamics of processes. For example, there might be a time delay between placing an order for raw materials and their arrival, affecting production schedules.

  By incorporating these elements, SD models provide a comprehensive and dynamic representation of complex systems, enabling analysts to simulate and study their behavior under various scenarios. This approach helps identify leverage points for intervention, predict long-term trends, and develop strategies for effective management and decision-making. System Dynamics is widely used in fields such as business, economics, environmental science, healthcare, and public policy to address complex issues and optimize system performance.

- **Agent-Based Modeling (ABM):** Agent-Based Modeling (ABM) is a versatile and powerful simulation technique that models the actions and interactions of autonomous agents, such as individuals, machines, or organizations, to assess their effects on the system as a whole. Each agent in the model operates according to a set of rules and behaviors, interacting with other agents and their environment in a way that reflects real-world dynamics. ABM is particularly useful for studying systems composed of heterogeneous entities with complex interactions, such as social systems, economic markets, and biological ecosystems.

  In ABM, agents are designed with distinct characteristics, decision-making processes, and behaviors that influence their interactions and responses to various stimuli. These interactions can lead to the emergence of complex system-level phenomena that are difficult to predict using traditional modeling approaches. For example, in a market simulation, individual consumers and producers may make decisions based on price changes, supply and demand, and personal preferences, leading to the emergence of market trends and economic patterns.

Applications in Industrial Engineering

1. **Manufacturing Systems:** Manufacturing systems benefit significantly from simulation and modeling, as these tools enable engineers to optimize production lines, reduce bottlenecks, and improve overall efficiency. By creating detailed virtual models of production processes, engineers can analyze and understand the interactions and dynamics within the system. This approach allows for the identification of inefficiencies and potential improvements without disrupting actual operations. Simulation and modeling enable the testing of various scenarios, such as changes in production schedules, the introduction of new machinery, or adjustments to workflow, providing valuable insights into their impact on overall performance. This proactive approach helps in making informed decisions, enhancing productivity, and ensuring a smooth and efficient manufacturing process. Ultimately, the use of simulation and modeling in manufacturing systems leads to better resource utilization, reduced downtime, and increased output, contributing to the organization's success and competitiveness.
2. **Supply Chain Management:** In supply chain management, simulation models play a crucial role in optimizing inventory levels, reducing lead

times, and improving service levels. These models provide a comprehensive representation of the entire supply chain, from suppliers to customers, allowing engineers to analyze and understand the complex interactions and dependencies within the system. By simulating different scenarios and strategies, engineers can identify inefficiencies, such as bottlenecks, delays, or excess inventory, and develop targeted solutions to address them.

Simulation models enable the testing of various inventory management approaches, such as just-in-time (JIT), safety stock, and reorder point strategies, helping to determine the optimal levels of inventory that balance holding costs and stockout risks. Additionally, these models can assess the impact of changes in supplier lead times, transportation routes, and demand patterns on overall supply chain performance.

Through the use of simulation, organizations can evaluate the effectiveness of different supply chain configurations, identify potential improvements, and make data-driven decisions to enhance efficiency and responsiveness. This approach not only helps in reducing costs and lead times but also ensures that customer demands are met consistently and effectively. Ultimately, simulation models provide valuable insights and actionable strategies for optimizing supply chain operations, leading to improved performance and competitive advantage.

3. **Logistics and Transportation:** In logistics and transportation, simulation plays a pivotal role in optimizing routes, managing fleets, and efficiently allocating resources. By creating detailed models of transportation networks, logistics companies can analyze and optimize various aspects of their operations, leading to significant improvements in performance and cost savings. For instance, simulation helps in identifying the most efficient delivery routes, considering factors such as traffic patterns, road conditions, and delivery schedules. This optimization reduces fuel consumption, minimizes travel time, and enhances overall delivery efficiency. Additionally, simulation aids in fleet management by modeling the deployment and utilization of vehicles, ensuring that the right resources are available at the right time and place. This approach enables companies to minimize idle time, reduce maintenance costs, and improve service levels. By leveraging simulation, logistics companies can test different scenarios, assess the impact of changes, and make data-driven decisions to enhance their

operations. Ultimately, simulation provides valuable insights and strategies for optimizing logistics and transportation, leading to improved efficiency, reduced costs, and higher customer satisfaction.

4. **Healthcare Systems:** In healthcare systems, industrial engineers play a crucial role in improving patient flow, optimizing resource allocation, and enhancing service delivery in hospitals through the use of simulation. By creating detailed models of different patient care scenarios, engineers can analyze the complexities of hospital operations and identify areas for improvement. These simulations help in understanding the interactions between various factors, such as patient arrivals, treatment processes, staff availability, and equipment usage.

   By simulating patient flow, engineers can develop strategies to reduce wait times and avoid bottlenecks in the system. For instance, they can test different scheduling approaches, evaluate the impact of increasing staff during peak hours, or explore the benefits of reorganizing treatment areas. These simulations allow for data-driven decision-making, ensuring that changes are implemented based on evidence rather than trial and error.

   Resource allocation is another critical area where simulation proves invaluable. Engineers can model the distribution of resources such as medical staff, equipment, and beds to ensure that they are used efficiently. This helps in optimizing the deployment of resources to meet patient demand while minimizing waste and costs.

   Additionally, simulation aids in enhancing service delivery by identifying and addressing potential issues before they occur. For example, engineers can simulate emergency department operations to predict the impact of a sudden influx of patients and develop contingency plans to maintain high-quality care.

   Overall, the use of simulation in healthcare systems enables hospitals to improve patient outcomes, increase operational efficiency, and deliver better quality care. By leveraging these tools, industrial engineers contribute to creating more effective and resilient healthcare systems that can adapt to changing demands and challenges.

5. **Energy Systems:** In the realm of energy systems, simulation and modeling are indispensable tools for designing and optimizing energy production and distribution networks. These techniques enable engineers to create detailed virtual representations of energy systems, allowing them to analyze and predict their performance under various

conditions. By simulating different energy demand scenarios, engineers can develop strategies to ensure a reliable and efficient energy supply. For instance, they can model the impact of fluctuating demand, renewable energy integration, and infrastructure changes on the overall system. This approach helps in identifying potential bottlenecks, assessing the feasibility of new technologies, and optimizing resource allocation. By using simulation and modeling, engineers can make informed decisions to enhance system reliability, reduce costs, and minimize environmental impact. Ultimately, these tools contribute to the development of robust and resilient energy systems that can adapt to changing demands and challenges, ensuring a sustainable energy future.

Tools and Software

- **AnyLogic:** AnyLogic is a versatile and powerful simulation modeling tool that supports multiple methodologies, including Discrete Event Simulation (DES), System Dynamics (SD), and Agent-Based Modeling (ABM). This multi-method approach allows users to create comprehensive and integrated models that capture the complexities of real-world systems more accurately.

  With AnyLogic, users can leverage the strengths of each modeling paradigm to address different aspects of a problem. For instance, DES is ideal for modeling processes and workflows that involve discrete events, such as manufacturing operations or logistics networks. SD, on the other hand, is well-suited for understanding the behavior of complex systems over time, incorporating feedback loops and time delays to represent the interactions within the system. ABM allows for the simulation of individual agents and their interactions, making it useful for studying systems with heterogeneous entities and complex dynamics, such as social systems or market behaviors.

  AnyLogic's intuitive interface and robust features enable users to build, analyze, and visualize models with ease. The tool provides a rich set of libraries and components, facilitating the rapid development of simulation models. Additionally, AnyLogic supports integration with various data sources and other software tools, enhancing its applicability in diverse fields such as healthcare, supply chain management, transportation, and energy systems.

By combining DES, SD, and ABM in a single platform, AnyLogic empowers users to tackle complex problems with a holistic approach, enabling more accurate predictions, better decision-making, and optimized outcomes. Its flexibility and comprehensive capabilities make AnyLogic an indispensable tool for simulation and modeling in industrial engineering and beyond.

- **FlexSim:** FlexSim is a cutting-edge software application designed for modeling, analyzing, and optimizing complex systems. This powerful tool is widely used across various industries, including manufacturing, healthcare, logistics, and supply chain management, to create accurate and dynamic simulations of real-world processes. FlexSim's intuitive interface and advanced features enable users to build detailed models with ease, allowing for the exploration and testing of different scenarios without disrupting actual operations.

  One of the key strengths of FlexSim is its ability to visualize complex systems through 3D animations and graphical representations. This feature provides a clear and comprehensive view of the system's behavior, helping users identify inefficiencies, bottlenecks, and opportunities for improvement. By using FlexSim, engineers and analysts can simulate different process configurations, evaluate the impact of changes, and develop optimized strategies to enhance overall performance.

  FlexSim also supports data integration and analysis, enabling users to input real-world data and generate meaningful insights. This capability allows for informed decision-making based on accurate and up-to-date information. Additionally, FlexSim offers a range of built-in tools and libraries, making it adaptable to various applications and industries.

  Overall, FlexSim is an invaluable tool for organizations seeking to improve their operations, reduce costs, and achieve their strategic objectives. By leveraging the power of simulation and modeling, FlexSim empowers users to optimize complex systems and drive continuous improvement.

- **Arena:** Arena is a comprehensive simulation software widely used for modeling, analyzing, and visualizing the operation of complex systems. It provides a robust platform for creating detailed and dynamic simulations that accurately represent real-world processes, allowing users to explore and optimize system performance without disrupting actual operations.

Arena's user-friendly interface and extensive libraries of pre-built modules enable users to build models quickly and efficiently. These modules cover various aspects of system operations, such as process flows, resource allocation, and interactions between components. By using Arena, engineers and analysts can simulate different scenarios, test the impact of changes, and identify areas for improvement.

One of the key strengths of Arena is its ability to visualize system behavior through animation and graphical representations. This feature provides a clear and intuitive understanding of how the system operates, helping users identify bottlenecks, inefficiencies, and potential solutions. The software also supports data integration and analysis, allowing users to input real-world data and generate meaningful insights.

Arena is widely used in industries such as manufacturing, healthcare, logistics, and service systems to optimize processes, reduce costs, and enhance overall performance. By leveraging the power of simulation, Arena empowers organizations to make informed decisions, improve operational efficiency, and achieve their strategic objectives. Its comprehensive capabilities make Arena an invaluable tool for anyone seeking to analyze and optimize the operation of complex systems.

Conclusion Simulation and modeling are critical components of industrial engineering, enabling engineers to design, analyze, and optimize systems in a virtual environment. By leveraging these tools, industrial engineers can improve the efficiency, reliability, and performance of complex systems across various industries.

CHAPTER FOURTEEN

DECISION ANALYSIS

Decision analysis is a systematic, quantitative, and visual approach to making high-quality decisions. It involves structuring and analyzing decision problems to identify the best course of action among alternatives. Key concepts include decision trees, which visually map out potential outcomes and their associated probabilities, and sensitivity analysis, which examines how changes in input variables affect the final decision. Techniques like Monte Carlo simulations are used to model and predict the impact of uncertainty, while tools such as multi-criteria decision analysis (MCDA) help weigh multiple factors and objectives. By employing these methods, decision-makers can objectively evaluate options, mitigate risks, and make informed choices that align with their goals and constraints.

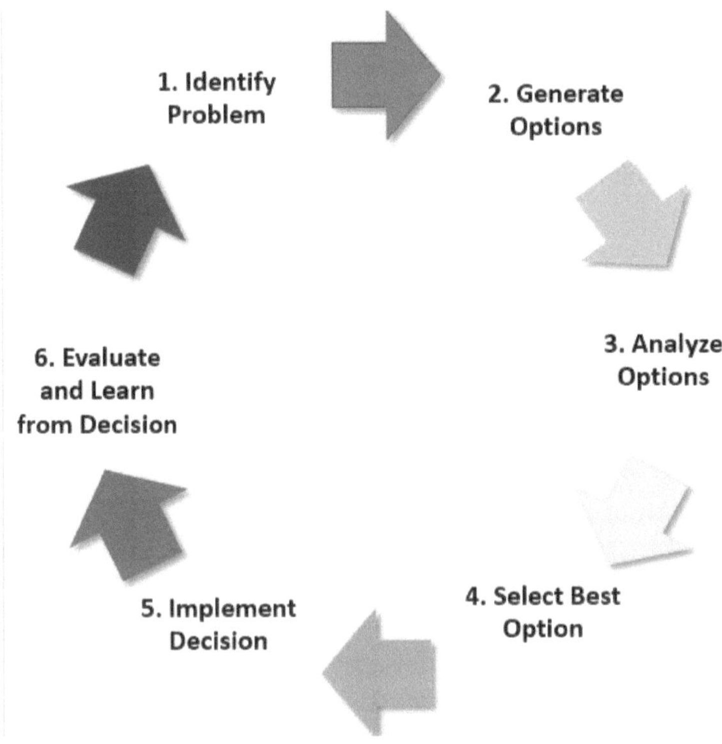

Decision Analysis

Here's a detailed look at the key concepts and techniques:

Introduction

Decision analysis provides a structured framework for making informed and logical choices by systematically evaluating the trade-offs between different decision options. This approach is particularly useful in situations where uncertainty and complexity are present, as it enables decision-makers to thoroughly assess potential outcomes and their associated risks. By breaking down complex decisions into manageable components, decision analysis facilitates a clear understanding of the various factors at play and their potential impact on the overall decision. It employs quantitative methods, such as decision trees, sensitivity analysis, and risk assessment, to evaluate the probabilities and consequences of different choices. Additionally, decision analysis integrates qualitative considerations, such as stakeholder preferences and values, to ensure a comprehensive evaluation. By combining both quantitative and qualitative insights, decision analysis helps identify the most advantageous course of action, leading to better and more confident decision-making. This systematic approach ultimately enhances the quality and effectiveness of decisions, particularly in complex and uncertain environments.

Key Concepts

1. **Decision Trees:** Decision Trees are an invaluable tool in decision analysis, providing a graphical representation of decision problems that illustrates the various decision paths, possible outcomes, and associated probabilities. These visual diagrams enable decision-makers to map out the sequence of choices and events, making it easier to understand the potential consequences of different decisions.

   A Decision Tree starts with a decision node, representing the initial choice to be made. From this node, branches extend to represent the possible decision alternatives. Each branch leads to either another decision node or a chance node, which signifies an event with multiple possible outcomes, each with an associated probability. These chance nodes further branch out to illustrate the potential consequences and subsequent decisions, forming a tree-like structure.

   By systematically breaking down the decision-making process into smaller, manageable components, Decision Trees help in evaluating the trade-offs between different options and identifying the most favorable course of action. They provide a clear and intuitive visualization of complex decision problems, making it easier to compare alternatives, assess risks, and make informed choices. Decision Trees are particularly useful in situations with uncertainty and multiple decision stages, as they enable a comprehensive analysis of the potential paths and their outcomes.

   Overall, Decision Trees facilitate better decision-making by offering a structured and transparent way to analyze and visualize the consequences of different decisions, ensuring that the best possible choice is made based on a thorough evaluation of all available information.
2. **Utility Theory:** Utility theory is a mathematical approach used to quantify preferences and make choices based on the expected utility of different outcomes. This theory assigns a numerical value, known as utility, to each possible outcome, reflecting the decision-maker's

subjective preferences, attitudes toward risk, and satisfaction levels. By evaluating and comparing these utility values, utility theory helps in ranking decision options based on their expected value, which is the sum of the utilities of all possible outcomes, weighted by their probabilities.

The core principle of utility theory is that decision-makers seek to maximize their expected utility rather than just the expected monetary value. This approach takes into account the varying degrees of satisfaction or dissatisfaction that different outcomes may bring. For example, a risk-averse individual may prefer a guaranteed but lower payoff over a high-risk, high-reward option, even if the latter has a higher expected monetary value. By incorporating individual preferences and risk attitudes, utility theory provides a more comprehensive and realistic framework for decision-making. It allows decision-makers to evaluate alternatives systematically, considering both the likelihood and the desirability of different outcomes. Ultimately, utility theory helps in making informed and rational choices that align with the decision-maker's goals and values, leading to better and more satisfying decision outcomes.

3. **Risk Analysis:** Risk analysis is a critical process that involves identifying, assessing, and managing the risks associated with different decision options. This process aims to evaluate the likelihood and impact of adverse outcomes to make informed and strategic decisions.

   The first step in risk analysis is identifying potential risks. This involves systematically exploring various scenarios and factors that could negatively affect the decision's outcome. Risks can stem from internal factors, such as operational inefficiencies, or external factors, such as market fluctuations and regulatory changes.

   Once potential risks are identified, the next step is assessing the likelihood and impact of each risk. This involves estimating the probability of each risk occurring and the severity of its consequences. Quantitative methods, such as statistical analysis and probability modeling, are often used to quantify the likelihood and impact of risks. Qualitative methods, such as expert judgment and scenario analysis, can also provide valuable insights.

   After assessing the risks, the focus shifts to managing and mitigating them. This involves developing strategies to reduce the likelihood and impact of adverse outcomes. Common risk management strategies include risk avoidance (eliminating the risk), risk reduction (implementing measures to minimize the risk), risk transfer (shifting the risk to another party, such as through insurance), and risk acceptance (acknowledging the risk and preparing to handle its consequences).

Effective risk analysis also involves continuous monitoring and review. As conditions change, new risks may emerge, and existing risks may evolve. Regularly updating the risk analysis ensures that decision-makers remain proactive and responsive to potential threats.

By systematically identifying, assessing, and managing risks, decision-makers can make more informed and resilient choices. Risk analysis provides a structured approach to navigating uncertainty, ensuring that potential adverse outcomes are considered and addressed, ultimately leading to better decision outcomes and improved organizational resilience.

4. **Sensitivity Analysis:** Sensitivity analysis is a vital technique in decision-making that involves examining how changes in input variables affect the outcomes of a decision. This process helps in understanding the robustness of a decision and identifying the critical factors that influence it. By systematically varying the input variables and observing the resulting changes in outcomes, sensitivity analysis provides insights into the dependencies and relationships within the decision-making process.

   One of the main benefits of sensitivity analysis is that it highlights which variables have the most significant impact on the decision outcome. This information enables decision-makers to focus on these key variables, ensuring that they are accurately estimated and well-managed. Additionally, sensitivity analysis helps in identifying potential risks and uncertainties, allowing for the development of strategies to mitigate them.

   For instance, in a business investment decision, sensitivity analysis can be used to assess how changes in market conditions, costs, or revenue projections affect the overall profitability of the investment. By understanding the range of possible outcomes and their associated probabilities, decision-makers can make more informed and resilient choices.

   Overall, sensitivity analysis enhances the quality of decision-making by providing a clearer understanding of the factors that drive outcomes and by enabling a more strategic approach to managing uncertainties and risks.

Techniques and Tools

1. **Multi-Criteria Decision Analysis (MCDA):** Multi-Criteria Decision Analysis (MCDA) is a sophisticated method for evaluating and prioritizing multiple decision options by considering various criteria. This approach is particularly useful when decisions involve balancing different objectives and making trade-offs between conflicting goals. By providing a structured framework for incorporating diverse criteria, MCDA helps decision-makers systematically analyze and compare alternatives.

   In MCDA, each decision option is assessed based on several criteria, which can be quantitative (e.g., cost, time) or qualitative (e.g., stakeholder satisfaction, environmental impact). These criteria are often weighted according to their relative importance, reflecting the decision-maker's priorities and preferences. MCDA facilitates a transparent and systematic decision-making process, allowing decision-makers to handle complex scenarios with multiple objectives and conflicting goals. By providing a clear framework for comparing alternatives, MCDA helps in making informed, balanced, and rational decisions that align with the decision-maker's priorities and values.
2. **Bayesian Analysis:** Bayesian Analysis is a powerful statistical approach that incorporates prior knowledge and evidence to update the probabilities of different outcomes. This method is grounded in Bayes' Theorem, which provides a mathematical framework for revising probabilities based on new information. By combining prior beliefs with empirical data, Bayesian Analysis offers a dynamic way to make decisions under uncertainty.

   Bayesian Analysis is particularly useful in situations with significant uncertainty, as it allows decision-makers to incorporate evolving evidence and adjust their understanding accordingly. For example, in medical research, Bayesian Analysis can be used to update the probability of a treatment's effectiveness as new clinical trial data emerges. In finance, it can help revise predictions of market trends based on recent economic indicators.

   Overall, Bayesian Analysis provides a robust and flexible framework for decision-making, enabling more accurate and adaptive responses to changing circumstances and new information.

3. **Decision Support Systems (DSS):** Decision Support Systems (DSS) are sophisticated, computer-based tools designed to assist in the decision-making process by providing relevant information, models, and analysis. These systems play a crucial role in organizing and analyzing complex decision problems, enabling decision-makers to evaluate alternatives, assess potential outcomes, and make informed choices.

   A DSS typically integrates various data sources, analytical models, and user-friendly interfaces to support decision-making. It provides users with the ability to retrieve, manipulate, and analyze data, as well as generate reports and visualizations that aid in understanding the implications of different options. By leveraging advanced computational capabilities, a DSS can handle large volumes of data and perform complex analyses that would be challenging to achieve manually.

Applications

- **Business and Finance:** In the realms of business and finance, decision analysis is a crucial tool for making informed and strategic decisions. It is extensively used for investment decisions, financial planning, risk management, and strategic planning. By systematically evaluating different scenarios and outcomes, decision analysis helps businesses identify the most advantageous courses of action to maximize value and achieve their objectives.

  In investment decisions, decision analysis enables investors to assess the potential risks and returns of various investment options. By considering factors such as market trends, economic conditions, and financial metrics, investors can make more informed choices that align with their risk tolerance and financial goals.

  Financial planning involves forecasting future financial performance, budgeting, and resource allocation. Decision analysis helps financial planners evaluate different financial strategies, such as savings plans, retirement funds, and debt management, to ensure long-term financial stability and growth.

  Risk management is another critical area where decision analysis plays a vital role. By identifying, assessing, and quantifying potential risks, businesses can develop strategies to mitigate and manage these risks. This includes analyzing the impact of adverse events, such as market downturns or supply chain disruptions, and implementing measures to minimize their effects.

In strategic planning, decision analysis supports the evaluation of different strategic initiatives, such as market expansion, product development, and mergers and acquisitions. By considering the potential outcomes and trade-offs of each option, businesses can make strategic decisions that align with their long-term vision and competitive positioning.

Overall, decision analysis provides a structured framework for evaluating complex decisions in business and finance. By incorporating both quantitative data and qualitative insights, it helps organizations make rational, data-driven decisions that maximize value and drive success.

- **Healthcare:** In healthcare, decision analysis is an invaluable tool used for medical diagnosis, treatment planning, and resource allocation. It provides a structured approach to assessing the benefits and risks of different medical interventions, enabling healthcare professionals to make informed choices that optimize patient outcomes. By integrating clinical data, patient preferences, and evidence-based guidelines, decision analysis helps in identifying the most effective treatment options tailored to individual patient needs.

  In medical diagnosis, decision analysis aids in evaluating the likelihood of various conditions based on symptoms, test results, and patient history. It helps clinicians weigh the probabilities and potential outcomes of different diagnostic pathways, ensuring accurate and timely identification of illnesses.

  For treatment planning, decision analysis allows healthcare providers to compare the effectiveness, risks, and costs of alternative treatments. By considering factors such as patient health status, potential side effects, and long-term outcomes, clinicians can develop personalized treatment plans that maximize benefits and minimize adverse effects.

  In the context of resource allocation, decision analysis helps healthcare organizations optimize the use of limited resources, such as hospital beds, medical equipment, and staff. By modeling different scenarios and evaluating their impact on patient care, decision-makers can prioritize interventions that deliver the highest value and improve overall healthcare efficiency.

  Ultimately, decision analysis in healthcare enhances the quality of care by providing a systematic and evidence-based approach to decision-making. It empowers healthcare professionals to make well-informed decisions that improve patient outcomes, reduce risks, and ensure the efficient use of resources.

- **Engineering and Design:** In the fields of engineering and design, decision analysis is an essential tool that aids in project management, product development, and system design. This systematic approach allows engineers to evaluate the trade-offs between cost, performance, and risk, enabling them to make informed and optimal design choices.

  Project Management Decision analysis helps project managers assess the feasibility, timelines, and resource requirements of various project options. By evaluating factors such as budget constraints, manpower, and potential risks, managers can prioritize tasks, allocate resources efficiently, and develop realistic project plans. This approach minimizes the likelihood of cost overruns, delays, and other project-related issues.

  Product Development In product development, decision analysis is used to compare different design concepts and prototypes. Engineers can assess the potential performance, manufacturing costs, and market acceptance of each option. This analysis helps in selecting the most promising design that meets customer needs, adheres to quality standards, and aligns with the company's strategic goals. Additionally, decision analysis can identify potential risks and uncertainties in the development process, allowing for proactive mitigation strategies.

  System Design For system design, decision analysis provides a framework for evaluating the trade-offs between various system configurations. Engineers can analyze the impact of different design choices on system performance, reliability, and maintainability. By considering factors such as component compatibility, redundancy, and scalability, engineers can design systems that meet the desired specifications while minimizing costs and risks.

  Overall, decision analysis enhances the quality and effectiveness of engineering and design decisions by providing a structured and quantitative approach to evaluating alternatives. It enables engineers to make data-driven choices that optimize performance, reduce risks, and ensure successful project outcomes. This approach ultimately leads to innovative and efficient solutions that meet the demands of modern engineering challenges.

- Public PolicyGovernments use decision analysis for policy development, resource allocation, and emergency planning. It helps in assessing the impact of different policy options and choosing the most beneficial course of action for society.

Conclusion

Decision analysis is a powerful tool that provides a structured approach to making informed and rational choices. By combining quantitative analysis with qualitative insights, decision-makers can evaluate the trade-offs between different options and make decisions that align with their goals and preferences.

CHAPTER FIFTEEN

Logistics and Distribution

Logistics and distribution are critical elements of supply chain management that ensure the seamless movement and delivery of goods from suppliers to customers. Effective logistics and distribution systems involve a series of coordinated activities, such as transportation management, inventory control, warehousing, and order fulfillment. These processes are designed to optimize the flow of goods, minimize costs, and meet customer expectations for timely delivery.

Transportation management is a key aspect of logistics, involving the planning, execution, and optimization of the movement of goods using various modes of transport, such as trucks, trains, ships, and airplanes. This ensures that goods are delivered efficiently and cost-effectively.

Inventory control focuses on maintaining optimal stock levels to meet customer demand without overstocking or understocking. This requires accurate demand forecasting, real-time tracking, and efficient replenishment strategies to minimize holding costs and reduce stockouts.

Warehousing involves the storage of goods until they are needed for production or distribution. Efficient warehouse management includes the design and layout of storage facilities, inventory control, and the use of technology to streamline operations and improve accuracy.

Order fulfillment encompasses the entire process of receiving, processing, and delivering customer orders. Efficient order fulfillment ensures that orders are accurately picked, packed, and shipped, leading to improved customer satisfaction and loyalty.

Overall, logistics and distribution play a pivotal role in supply chain management, ensuring that goods are delivered efficiently and effectively, ultimately contributing to the success and competitiveness of businesses. By optimizing these processes, companies can reduce costs, improve service levels, and enhance customer satisfaction.

Key Concepts in Logistics and Distribution:

1. Transportation Management: Transportation management is a critical component of logistics that involves a series of strategic decisions and actions to ensure the efficient movement of goods. It encompasses several key aspects, including routing and scheduling to determine the most efficient routes and schedules for transportation, carrier selection to choose the appropriate transportation providers based on cost, reliability, and delivery speed, and load planning to organize and optimize the loading of goods onto transport vehicles. Additionally, it involves freight consolidation to combine multiple shipments into a single transport, shipment tracking to monitor the movement of goods in real-time, compliance management to ensure adherence to relevant regulations and standards, and risk management to identify and mitigate potential risks associated with transportation. By effectively managing these aspects, transportation management ensures that goods are delivered efficiently, cost-effectively, and reliably, ultimately contributing to the overall success of the supply chain. It encompasses several key aspects:

- **Mode Selection:** Mode selection is a crucial aspect of transportation management that involves choosing the most appropriate mode of transportation—such as road, rail, air, or sea—based on factors like cost, speed, distance, and the nature of the goods being transported. Each mode offers distinct advantages and trade-offs. For example, air transport is ideal for high-value, time-sensitive products due to its speed, despite higher costs. Conversely, sea transport is more suitable for bulk goods with less urgency, as it offers cost efficiency for large volumes but takes longer. Road transport is often used for short to medium distances with flexible scheduling, while rail transport provides an efficient solution for heavy goods over longer distances. By carefully evaluating these factors, businesses can optimize their logistics operations, balancing cost and efficiency to meet specific delivery requirements.
- **Route Optimization:** Route optimization is a pivotal aspect of transportation management that involves meticulously planning the most efficient paths to minimize transportation costs and reduce delivery times. This intricate process requires the analysis of numerous

factors, including real-time traffic conditions, road infrastructure quality, fuel consumption rates, and precise delivery schedules. By leveraging advanced technologies and sophisticated algorithms, companies can optimize routes, factoring in dynamic variables such as weather conditions and potential delays. These technologies help ensure that goods are transported via the shortest and fastest routes, maximizing efficiency and cost-effectiveness. Ultimately, effective route optimization not only improves delivery speed but also enhances overall operational efficiency and customer satisfaction.

- **Fleet Management:** Fleet management is a critical aspect of transportation management, focusing on the coordination and administration of a fleet of vehicles to ensure timely and cost-effective delivery. It encompasses a range of activities, including scheduling regular maintenance to keep vehicles in optimal condition and prevent breakdowns, monitoring vehicle performance to track fuel efficiency and detect potential issues early, and managing driver assignments to optimize workload and routes. Additionally, fleet management involves ensuring compliance with safety regulations and standards to maintain a safe operating environment. By effectively managing these aspects, fleet managers can maximize the utilization of vehicles, reduce operational costs through efficient fuel management and maintenance practices, and enhance overall delivery performance. This comprehensive approach not only improves the reliability of the transportation network but also contributes to increased customer satisfaction and operational efficiency.

2. Warehouse Management: Warehouse management is a pivotal component of logistics that ensures the efficient storage, handling, and movement of goods within a warehouse facility. This intricate process involves several key activities aimed at maintaining smooth operations and effectively meeting customer demands. One of the primary activities is inventory management, which includes tracking stock levels, forecasting demand, and implementing strategies to prevent stockouts or overstocking. Another crucial aspect is the organization of storage space to maximize efficiency and accessibility, often achieved through the use of advanced warehouse management systems (WMS) and automation technologies. Additionally, order fulfillment processes are optimized to ensure accurate and timely picking, packing, and shipping of goods. Warehouse management also entails ensuring the safety and security of both goods and personnel by adhering to safety regulations and implementing robust security measures. By effectively managing these activities, warehouse operations can achieve higher efficiency, reduce costs, and enhance overall customer satisfaction.

- **Inventory Control:** Inventory control is a crucial aspect of logistics management, focusing on maintaining optimal stock levels to balance supply and demand. Effective inventory control involves the precise tracking of inventory through accurate record-keeping and barcode scanning systems, which enable real-time monitoring of stock levels. By leveraging inventory management software, businesses can forecast future demand based on historical data and market trends, ensuring that stock levels are aligned with expected sales. This proactive approach minimizes holding costs associated with excess inventory and reduces the risk of stockouts, which can lead to lost sales and customer dissatisfaction. Additionally, inventory control practices help in identifying slow-moving or obsolete items, allowing businesses to take corrective actions such as discounting or discontinuation. Overall, efficient inventory control ensures that products are available when needed, enhances customer satisfaction, and keeps operational costs in check, contributing to the overall success of the supply chain.
- **Storage Solutions:** Storage solutions are a fundamental aspect of warehouse management, focusing on designing efficient layouts and storage systems to optimize space utilization and ease of access. Selecting the appropriate storage methods, such as shelving, pallet racking, or mezzanine floors, plays a pivotal role in accommodating various types of goods based on their size, weight, and demand frequency. Implementing efficient storage solutions involves categorizing and organizing items in a systematic manner, often using automated systems like vertical lift modules or automated storage and retrieval systems (AS/RS) to further enhance space utilization and operational efficiency. Additionally, employing techniques such as cross-docking and batch picking can streamline the flow of goods within the warehouse, reducing handling times and labor costs. By optimizing storage solutions, businesses can significantly improve their overall productivity, ensure quick and accurate order fulfillment, and maintain a well-organized and efficient warehouse environment.

- **Order Fulfillment:** Order fulfillment is a critical process in logistics that involves picking, packing, and shipping orders to meet customer expectations. This complex operation requires precise coordination and execution to ensure orders are accurately picked from inventory, securely packed to prevent damage during transit, and dispatched promptly to meet delivery timelines. Efficient order fulfillment hinges on the integration of advanced technologies such as barcode scanning, which ensures accurate tracking and inventory management, and automated picking systems, which speed up the process and reduce human error. Additionally, real-time tracking and updates provide customers with transparency and assurance about their order status. By optimizing the order fulfillment process, businesses can enhance speed and accuracy, leading to higher customer satisfaction, increased loyalty, and a competitive edge in the market.

By focusing on these key aspects, warehouse management plays a vital role in ensuring the smooth operation of the supply chain, ultimately contributing to the success and competitiveness of the business. Properly managed warehouses lead to cost savings, improved efficiency, and better customer service.

3. Distribution Networks: Distribution networks are essential for ensuring the efficient movement of goods from suppliers to customers, employing a variety of strategies and techniques to optimize the flow of products, reduce costs, and meet customer expectations. These networks involve a series of interconnected nodes, including warehouses, distribution centers, and transportation hubs, strategically located to minimize transit times and transportation costs. Effective distribution network design incorporates demand forecasting and inventory management to ensure the right products are available at the right locations, reducing the risk of stockouts or overstocking. Advanced technologies, such as geographic information systems (GIS) and transportation management systems (TMS), aid in planning and optimizing routes, while collaborative relationships with logistics partners enhance efficiency and reliability. By continuously analyzing and adapting distribution strategies, businesses can streamline their supply chains, improve service levels, and maintain a competitive edge in the market.

- **Centralized vs. Decentralized:** One of the critical decisions in designing a distribution network is choosing between a centralized and decentralized approach. A centralized distribution network consolidates inventory and operations into a single, central distribution center. This method often results in economies of scale, as it allows businesses to reduce overall costs through bulk purchasing, streamlined operations, and centralized management. However, this approach can lead to longer lead times and reduced flexibility in meeting regional demands, as all goods must be transported from the central hub to various destinations.

  On the other hand, a decentralized distribution network involves multiple regional centers strategically located closer to customers. This approach can significantly improve service levels by reducing lead times and providing more responsive and flexible delivery options. By placing inventory closer to the end customers, businesses can quickly adapt to regional demand fluctuations and ensure timely deliveries. However, decentralization may increase overall costs due to the need for multiple facilities, increased management complexity, and potential duplication of resources.

  The choice between centralized and decentralized distribution depends on various factors, including cost considerations, desired service levels, lead time requirements, and the nature of the products being distributed. Businesses must carefully evaluate these factors to determine the most suitable distribution network design that aligns with their operational goals and customer expectations.
- **Cross-Docking:** Cross-docking is a highly efficient logistics technique that involves the direct transfer of incoming goods to outgoing vehicles with minimal or no storage time in between. This approach significantly reduces storage and handling costs, as products spend less time sitting in warehouses. By eliminating the need for prolonged storage, cross-docking minimizes the risk of inventory obsolescence and spoilage, making it particularly beneficial for perishable goods, high-demand items, and products with short lead times. The streamlined flow of goods through cross-docking enables faster delivery times and enhances overall supply chain efficiency. Advanced technologies such as automated sorting systems and real-time tracking can further optimize the cross-docking process, ensuring that goods are accurately directed to their final destinations. As a result, businesses can reduce inventory holding costs, improve order fulfillment speed, and boost customer

satisfaction through timely and reliable deliveries.

- **Last Mile Delivery:** Last mile delivery is the final and often most challenging leg of the delivery process, involving the efficient and timely delivery of goods to their final destination, typically the customer's doorstep. This stage is particularly complex and costly due to factors such as traffic congestion, varying delivery locations, and the necessity for precise timing to meet customer expectations. To optimize last mile delivery, businesses employ strategies such as route optimization, which involves using advanced algorithms to plan the most efficient delivery routes, and the establishment of local delivery hubs to shorten the distance between distribution centers and customers. Leveraging technology like GPS tracking allows for real-time monitoring of delivery vehicles, ensuring better route planning and timely deliveries. Additionally, automated delivery systems, including drones and autonomous vehicles, are being explored to further enhance the efficiency of last mile delivery. Efficient last mile delivery is crucial for maintaining customer satisfaction, as timely and accurate deliveries significantly impact the overall customer experience and help businesses maintain a competitive edge in the market.

1. Just-in-Time (JIT) Delivery:

- **Minimizing Inventory:** Minimizing inventory is an essential strategy in logistics management that focuses on reducing stock levels by synchronizing deliveries with production schedules. This approach aims to decrease holding costs, which include expenses related to storage, insurance, and obsolescence. By aligning inventory replenishment with actual production needs, businesses can maintain optimal stock levels, ensuring that materials and products are available when required without overstocking. This synchronization often involves the implementation of just-in-time (JIT) inventory systems, where deliveries are timed to arrive precisely when needed in the production process. Advanced forecasting and inventory management tools help businesses accurately predict demand and adjust their supply chain operations accordingly. By minimizing inventory, companies can increase efficiency, reduce waste, and enhance overall profitability while maintaining the ability to meet customer demands promptly.

- **Demand Forecasting:** Demand forecasting is a vital practice in supply chain management that involves using data and advanced analytics to predict customer demand and plan deliveries accordingly. By analyzing historical sales data, market trends, seasonal variations, and other relevant factors, businesses can create accurate demand forecasts that inform production schedules and inventory management. Advanced technologies such as machine learning and artificial intelligence enhance the precision of these forecasts by identifying complex patterns and relationships within the data. Effective demand forecasting allows companies to align their supply chain operations with actual market demand, reducing the risk of stockouts or overstocking, optimizing inventory levels, and improving overall operational efficiency. This proactive approach also enables businesses to respond swiftly to changes in customer preferences and market conditions, ensuring they can meet customer expectations while minimizing costs and maximizing profitability.

2. E-Commerce and Retail:

Omni-Channel Distribution: Omni-channel distribution is a strategic approach that integrates both online and offline channels to provide a seamless and cohesive customer experience. This method ensures that customers can interact with a brand through various touchpoints, such as physical stores, e-commerce websites, mobile apps, and social media platforms, without any disruption or inconsistency. By synchronizing inventory, order fulfillment, and customer service across these channels, businesses can offer a unified shopping experience where customers can effortlessly switch between online and offline interactions. For example, a customer might browse products online, check availability in a nearby store, make a purchase on a mobile app, and choose to pick up the item in-store. Advanced technologies, such as integrated point-of-sale (POS) systems, real-time inventory tracking, and customer relationship management (CRM) software, play a crucial role in facilitating omni-channel distribution. By adopting this approach, businesses can enhance customer satisfaction, increase sales, and build long-term loyalty by providing a consistent and convenient shopping experience across all channels.

Fulfillment Centers: Fulfillment centers are strategically located warehouses designed to efficiently process and ship online orders, playing a crucial role in the e-commerce supply chain. These centers are equipped with advanced technology and systems to handle large volumes of orders, ensuring quick and accurate order fulfillment. The location of fulfillment centers is carefully chosen to be close to major population centers, transportation hubs, and distribution networks, reducing shipping times and costs. Inside these centers, products are stored, picked, packed, and shipped using automated systems, such as conveyor belts, robotics, and barcode scanners, to streamline operations and minimize errors. By optimizing the layout and processes within fulfillment centers, businesses can significantly enhance their order processing speed, improve inventory management, and provide a seamless shopping experience for customers. Efficient fulfillment centers help companies meet the growing demands of online shoppers, ensuring timely deliveries and boosting customer satisfaction.

3. Global Logistics:

- **International Shipping:** International shipping involves navigating the intricate landscape of cross-border transportation, encompassing customs regulations, tariffs, and international trade agreements. Managing these complexities requires a thorough understanding of the regulatory environment in both the exporting and importing countries. Customs regulations dictate the documentation and procedures necessary for goods to enter or leave a country, while tariffs impose duties on imported goods based on their value, origin, and classification. Additionally, international trade agreements between countries can influence tariff rates, trade barriers, and compliance requirements.

  To effectively handle international shipping, businesses must ensure accurate documentation, such as invoices, packing lists, and certificates of origin, to comply with customs requirements. They must also calculate and pay the appropriate tariffs, which may vary depending on the product and trade agreements in place. Partnering with experienced freight forwarders and customs brokers can help streamline the process, ensuring that shipments adhere to all regulations and reach their destinations efficiently. Advanced tracking and communication technologies provide real-time updates on shipment status, helping businesses anticipate and address any potential delays or issues. By expertly managing the complexities of international shipping, companies can expand their global reach, optimize supply chain operations, and deliver products to customers worldwide.

- **Supply Chain Visibility:** Supply chain visibility involves the use of advanced technologies to track and monitor goods throughout the entire supply chain, ensuring transparency and efficiency at every stage. By implementing solutions such as RFID (Radio Frequency Identification) tags, IoT (Internet of Things) sensors, and GPS tracking, businesses can gain real-time insights into the location and status of their products, from production to delivery. This enhanced visibility allows for better coordination and decision-making, as stakeholders can quickly identify and address potential issues, such as delays, disruptions, or inventory shortages. Additionally, supply chain visibility tools provide valuable data for analyzing performance metrics, optimizing processes, and improving overall operational efficiency. With transparent and efficient supply chain management, companies can enhance customer satisfaction by providing accurate and timely information about order status and delivery times, ultimately building trust and loyalty.

Technological Advancements:

1. **Warehouse Automation:** Warehouse automation involves the implementation of robotics and automated systems to significantly boost efficiency and accuracy in warehouse operations. By integrating technologies such as autonomous mobile robots (AMRs), automated guided vehicles (AGVs), and robotic picking systems, warehouses can streamline various tasks including inventory management, order picking, packing, and sorting. These automated systems reduce the reliance on manual labor, minimizing human error and enhancing the speed of operations. Advanced software and machine learning algorithms help in optimizing the movement and handling of goods, ensuring precise and efficient workflows. Additionally, automation contributes to improved safety by reducing the risk of accidents associated with manual handling of heavy or hazardous materials. By leveraging warehouse automation, businesses can achieve higher throughput, reduce operational costs, and maintain a competitive edge in an increasingly fast-paced logistics environment.
2. **Internet of Things (IoT):** The Internet of Things (IoT) is revolutionizing the logistics industry by providing real-time tracking and monitoring of shipments, improving inventory management, and enhancing overall supply chain visibility. IoT devices, such as sensors, RFID tags, and GPS

trackers, are embedded in goods, containers, and transport vehicles to collect and transmit data throughout the supply chain. This continuous flow of information enables businesses to monitor the location, condition, and status of shipments in real time, providing valuable insights for proactive decision-making. For example, temperature sensors can ensure that perishable goods are transported under optimal conditions, while GPS trackers can provide precise location updates to optimize delivery routes and schedules. Additionally, IoT-enabled inventory management systems offer real-time visibility into stock levels, reducing the risk of stockouts or overstocking. By integrating IoT technology, companies can enhance operational efficiency, reduce costs, and improve customer satisfaction through timely and accurate information. The ability to quickly identify and address potential issues also strengthens the resilience and responsiveness of the supply chain, making it more adaptable to changing market demands.

3. **Artificial Intelligence (AI):** Artificial Intelligence (AI) is revolutionizing logistics operations by providing advanced tools for demand forecasting, route optimization, and decision-making. By leveraging AI algorithms and machine learning models, businesses can analyze vast amounts of data to predict customer demand with high accuracy. This enables more efficient inventory management and production planning, reducing the risk of stockouts and overstocking. For route optimization, AI algorithms consider various factors such as traffic conditions, weather, and delivery schedules to determine the most efficient paths, reducing transportation costs and delivery times. Additionally, AI-powered decision-making tools help logistics managers make informed choices by analyzing real-time data and identifying patterns and trends. These tools can assist in selecting the best carriers, optimizing warehouse operations, and managing risks. By harnessing the power of AI, logistics operations become more efficient, cost-effective, and responsive to changing market demands, ultimately enhancing customer satisfaction and competitiveness.

Conclusion:

Logistics and distribution are fundamental to the success of any supply chain. By optimizing transportation, warehouse management, and distribution networks, companies can significantly improve operational efficiency, reduce costs, and enhance customer satisfaction. Efficient transportation management ensures timely delivery of goods, while effective warehouse management streamlines storage and handling processes, reducing inventory costs and increasing order fulfillment speed. Additionally, well-designed distribution networks enable companies to strategically position their products closer to customers, further reducing lead times and improving service levels. Technological advancements, such as artificial intelligence, the Internet of Things (IoT), and warehouse automation, are continuously reshaping the logistics landscape. These innovations provide real-time visibility, predictive analytics, and automated solutions, enabling businesses to make data-driven decisions and respond swiftly to market changes. As technology continues to evolve, the logistics field presents endless possibilities for enhancing supply chain performance, driving growth, and maintaining a competitive edge.

CHAPTER SIXTEEN

SUPPLY CHAIN DESIGN AND OPTIMIZATION

Supply chain design and optimization are essential for creating efficient, resilient, and cost-effective supply chains. This process involves several key concepts, strategies, and tools to ensure that all elements of the supply chain work harmoniously to meet business objectives and customer needs. One of the primary concepts is network design, which involves determining the optimal number and location of facilities such as factories, warehouses, and distribution centers to minimize costs and improve service levels.

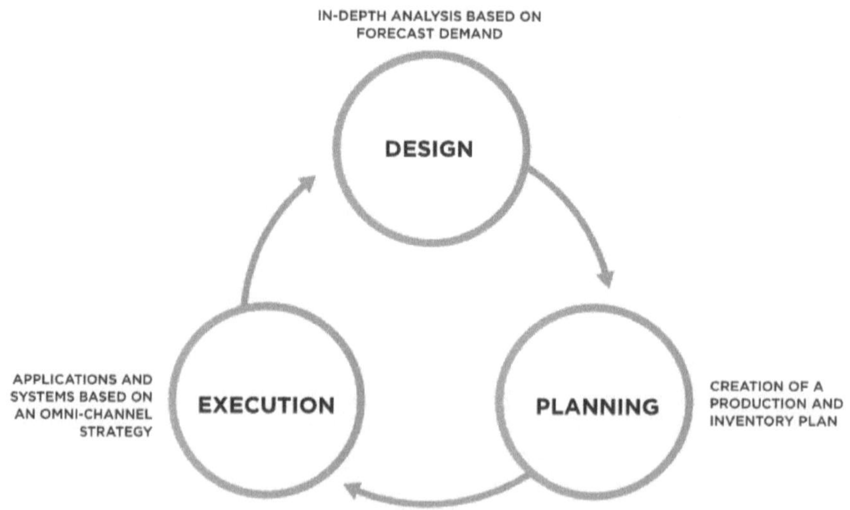

Supply Chain Design and Optimization

Supply chain segmentation is another critical strategy, where different segments of the supply chain are tailored to meet the distinct needs of various customer groups, products, or markets. This helps in aligning supply chain capabilities with specific business requirements, enhancing overall efficiency and responsiveness.

Advanced analytical tools and technologies play a vital role in supply chain optimization. Supply chain modeling and simulation allow businesses to create digital representations of their supply chains, enabling them to test different scenarios, identify potential bottlenecks, and evaluate the impact of changes before implementation. Optimization algorithms are used to solve complex problems such as inventory management, transportation planning, and production scheduling, ensuring that resources are utilized effectively and costs are minimized.

Collaborative planning, forecasting, and replenishment (CPFR) is a strategy that involves close cooperation between supply chain partners to share information and align their operations. This collaborative approach enhances visibility, reduces uncertainties, and improves overall supply chain performance.

By leveraging these key concepts, strategies, and tools, businesses can design and optimize their supply chains to be more efficient, resilient, and cost-effective, ultimately driving growth and customer satisfaction in an increasingly competitive market.

Let's explore the key concepts, strategies, and tools involved in this process:

Key Concepts in Supply Chain Design and Optimization:

1. Supply Chain Network Design:

- **Network Structure:** Network structure is a fundamental aspect of supply chain design, involving the strategic planning of the number and location of various components, such as suppliers, manufacturing facilities, distribution centers, and customers. This process aims to create an efficient and cost-effective network that optimally balances production and distribution. The selection of suppliers is critical, as it influences the availability, quality, and cost of raw materials. Manufacturing facilities must be strategically located to minimize production costs and transit times while maintaining proximity to key markets. Distribution centers should be positioned to ensure timely delivery and efficient logistics, reducing transportation costs and lead times. Additionally, understanding the geographical distribution of customers is essential for determining the optimal placement of these nodes. Advanced modeling and optimization tools help businesses analyze various scenarios and make data-driven decisions, ensuring that the network structure aligns with operational goals and customer demands. By designing an effective network structure, companies can enhance their supply chain's resilience, flexibility, and overall performance, ultimately contributing to customer satisfaction and competitive advantage.

- **Network Configuration:** Network configuration is a critical aspect of supply chain design that involves determining the most efficient and cost-effective arrangement of supply chain elements to meet service level requirements. This process includes evaluating and selecting the number and locations of suppliers, manufacturing facilities, distribution centers, and warehouses. The goal is to minimize overall costs, including production, transportation, and inventory holding costs, while ensuring that customer service levels, such as delivery speed and reliability, are met.

  Advanced analytical tools and optimization algorithms are often employed to model various network configurations and assess their impact on supply chain performance. Factors such as demand patterns, transportation costs, lead times, and capacity constraints are taken into account to identify the optimal configuration. Sensitivity analysis can also be conducted to understand how changes in these factors might affect the network's efficiency.

  By optimizing the network configuration, businesses can achieve a balance between cost reduction and high service levels, enabling them to respond more effectively to market demands and maintain a competitive edge. This strategic approach ensures that the supply chain is both resilient and adaptable, capable of delivering value to customers while optimizing operational efficiency.

- **Supply Chain Integration:** Supply chain integration is a crucial aspect of logistics management that focuses on ensuring the seamless integration of all components within the supply chain to achieve smooth and efficient operations. This involves the coordination and synchronization of various processes, including procurement, production, transportation, warehousing, and distribution, to create a unified and cohesive supply chain. Effective supply chain integration relies on advanced technologies such as Enterprise Resource Planning (ERP) systems, which provide real-time visibility and control over all supply chain activities. By sharing accurate and timely information across all stakeholders, including suppliers, manufacturers, and distributors, businesses can enhance collaboration and reduce inefficiencies. This integrated approach helps in minimizing delays, reducing costs, and improving overall responsiveness to market demands. Additionally, supply chain integration fosters better risk management by enabling companies to quickly identify and address potential disruptions. By achieving seamless integration, businesses can optimize their supply chain performance, enhance customer satisfaction, and maintain a competitive advantage in the market.

2. Optimization Techniques: Optimization techniques are essential methods used in logistics and supply chain management to enhance efficiency, reduce costs, and improve overall performance. These techniques involve various mathematical and algorithmic approaches to determine the most effective solutions for complex problems. Linear programming, integer programming, and mixed-integer linear programming are commonly used for optimizing production schedules, transportation planning, and inventory management. Heuristic methods, such as genetic algorithms and simulated annealing, provide approximate solutions for problems that are computationally infeasible with exact methods. Dynamic programming is effective for multi-stage decision-making processes, while stochastic optimization accounts for uncertainty and variability. Network optimization and simulation modeling help design and evaluate supply chain networks and strategies. By applying these optimization techniques, businesses can make data-driven decisions, enhance operational efficiency, and maintain a competitive edge in the market.

- **Linear Programming:** Linear programming is a mathematical method employed to determine the optimal outcome in a given model with linear relationships. This technique involves formulating a problem as a set of linear equations and inequalities, where the objective is to maximize or minimize a linear function, known as the objective function. Linear programming is widely used in logistics and supply chain management for optimizing various operations, including production schedules, transportation planning, and inventory management. For example, in production scheduling, linear programming helps determine the most efficient allocation of resources to meet production targets while minimizing costs. In transportation planning, it assists in finding the optimal routes and schedules to reduce transportation costs and delivery times. For inventory management, linear programming can be used to balance stock levels, minimize holding costs, and ensure timely replenishment. By leveraging linear programming, businesses can make data-driven decisions that enhance operational efficiency, reduce costs, and improve overall supply chain performance.

- **Integer Programming:** Integer programming is an advanced mathematical optimization technique that extends linear programming by requiring some or all decision variables to be integers. This method is particularly suitable for modeling scenarios where decisions involve discrete choices, such as the selection of facility locations, staffing levels, or production quantities. Unlike linear programming, which allows for continuous variables, integer programming ensures that solutions are practical and applicable to real-world situations where fractional values are not feasible.

  For instance, in the context of facility location, integer programming can help determine the optimal number and placement of warehouses or distribution centers to minimize costs and meet service level requirements. Similarly, it can be used to decide on the number of employees needed for specific shifts or the quantity of products to be produced in discrete units. Integer programming models often involve binary variables (0 or 1) to represent decisions such as whether to open a facility or not.

  By leveraging integer programming, businesses can make more precise and realistic decisions, optimizing their operations and improving overall efficiency. This approach is invaluable for tackling complex logistical problems where discrete choices play a significant role in determining the best possible outcomes.
- **Heuristic Methods:** Heuristic methods are advanced techniques employed to solve complex optimization problems that are computationally infeasible with exact methods. These techniques provide approximate solutions in a reasonable timeframe, making them valuable for tackling large-scale and intricate problems. Genetic algorithms are inspired by the process of natural selection, utilizing

mechanisms such as selection, crossover, and mutation to evolve a population of potential solutions over successive generations. This approach helps identify near-optimal solutions by exploring a wide search space and avoiding local optima.

Simulated annealing, on the other hand, is inspired by the annealing process in metallurgy, where a material is gradually cooled to reach a stable state. In this method, a solution is iteratively improved by making small changes and accepting or rejecting them based on a probabilistic acceptance criterion. The probability of accepting worse solutions decreases over time, allowing the algorithm to escape local optima and converge to a global optimum.

Both genetic algorithms and simulated annealing are particularly effective for solving complex optimization problems in logistics, such as vehicle routing, facility location, and production scheduling. By leveraging these heuristic methods, businesses can find practical and efficient solutions to problems that would be otherwise computationally prohibitive to solve with exact methods, ultimately enhancing their operational efficiency and decision-making capabilities.

3. Demand Forecasting: Demand forecasting is an essential component of supply chain management that involves predicting future customer demand using data and analytics. By analyzing historical sales data, market trends, seasonal patterns, and other relevant factors, businesses can create accurate forecasts that inform production, inventory, and distribution planning. Advanced technologies such as machine learning and artificial intelligence enhance the precision of demand forecasts by identifying complex patterns and relationships within the data. Effective demand forecasting enables companies to align their supply chain operations with actual market demand, reducing the risk of stockouts or overstocking. This proactive approach ensures optimal inventory levels, minimizes costs, and improves overall operational efficiency. Additionally, accurate demand forecasting allows businesses to respond swiftly to changes in customer preferences and market conditions, ensuring they can meet customer expectations and maintain a competitive edge in the market.

- **Statistical Methods:** Statistical methods involve the use of historical data and statistical techniques to predict future demand accurately. By analyzing past sales records, customer behavior patterns, market trends, and other relevant factors, businesses can identify patterns and relationships that help forecast future demand. Techniques such as time series analysis, regression analysis, and moving averages are commonly employed to model and predict demand variations over time. Time series analysis focuses on identifying patterns like seasonality, trends, and cyclic behavior in historical data, while regression analysis examines the relationships between demand and influencing factors. Moving averages smooth out short-term fluctuations to highlight longer-term trends. By leveraging these statistical methods, companies can make informed decisions about production planning, inventory management, and resource allocation, ultimately enhancing operational efficiency and meeting customer demands more effectively.

- **Machine Learning:** Machine learning leverages advanced algorithms to significantly improve the accuracy of demand forecasts by identifying complex patterns and trends within data. By analyzing vast amounts of historical data, machine learning models can uncover hidden relationships and correlations that traditional statistical methods might miss. These algorithms, such as neural networks, decision trees, and support vector machines, continuously learn and adapt to new data, refining their predictions over time. Machine learning techniques can account for various factors influencing demand, including seasonality, promotional activities, and market conditions. Additionally, they can handle non-linear and multi-dimensional data, providing more precise and granular forecasts. By incorporating machine learning into demand forecasting processes, businesses can make more informed decisions, optimize inventory levels, reduce costs, and better meet customer demands, ultimately enhancing overall supply chain performance.

4. Strategies for Supply Chain Design and Optimization: Strategies for supply chain design and optimization encompass a range of methodologies and best practices aimed at enhancing the efficiency, resilience, and cost-effectiveness of supply chain operations. These strategies involve a comprehensive approach to network design, inventory management, integration, and risk management, among other aspects. The goal is to create a supply chain that can adapt to changing market demands, minimize costs, and deliver high levels of customer service. Key components include the strategic placement of facilities, effective inventory control, seamless integration of supply chain partners, and the adoption of advanced technologies. Additionally, optimizing supply chain operations through techniques such as linear programming, heuristic methods, and demand forecasting enables businesses to make data-driven decisions that enhance overall performance. By implementing these strategies, companies can achieve a competitive edge, ensure timely deliveries, and maintain customer satisfaction. Key strategies include:

Centralized vs. Decentralized Supply Chains: Centralized and decentralized supply chains represent two different approaches to managing the flow of goods and services within an organization.

- **Centralized Supply Chain:** Centralized supply chains are characterized by a centralized control structure, where decision-making and inventory management are consolidated at a single location, often the company's headquarters or a central distribution center. This approach allows for greater standardization, consistent policies, and better economies of scale, as the organization can negotiate better rates with suppliers due to bulk purchasing. Centralized supply chains often lead to reduced operational costs and improved coordination, as all processes are streamlined through a single point of control. However, this model can also result in longer lead times and reduced flexibility in responding to local market demands or disruptions.
- **Decentralized Supply Chain:** Decentralized supply chains, on the other hand, distribute decision-making and inventory management across multiple locations, such as regional or local warehouses and distribution centers. This approach offers greater flexibility and responsiveness to local market conditions, allowing businesses to quickly adapt to changes in demand and address disruptions more effectively. Decentralized supply chains can provide faster delivery times and improved customer service, as products are stored closer to the end customers. However, this model can lead to higher operational costs due to duplicated efforts and reduced economies of scale, as each location may have its own procurement and inventory management processes.

5. Inventory Optimization: Inventory optimization is the strategic process of determining the optimal inventory levels to meet customer demand while minimizing costs and maximizing efficiency. It involves balancing the costs associated with holding inventory, such as storage, insurance, and obsolescence, with the costs of stockouts, such as lost sales and customer dissatisfaction. Effective inventory optimization ensures that businesses maintain the right amount of stock to fulfill orders promptly without overstocking or understocking.

- **Safety Stock Management:** Safety stock management is the process of determining the optimal level of extra inventory, known as safety stock, to protect against uncertainties in demand and supply. The primary goal is to balance the risk of stockouts, which can lead to lost sales and dissatisfied customers, with the cost of holding additional inventory. To achieve this balance, businesses must consider factors such as demand variability, lead time variability, and the desired service level. Calculating safety stock typically involves statistical methods that account for these factors, such as using standard deviation and z-scores to determine the appropriate buffer. Effective safety stock management ensures that companies can maintain a steady supply of products to meet customer demand, even in the face of unforeseen disruptions, while minimizing the costs associated with excess inventory. This strategic approach helps improve overall supply chain resilience and customer satisfaction.
- **Reorder Point Calculation:** Reorder point calculation is a fundamental aspect of inventory management that involves establishing the optimal points at which to reorder inventory to ensure a continuous supply of products while minimizing the risk of stockouts and excess inventory. The reorder point is determined based on two critical factors: lead times and demand variability. Lead times refer to the duration it takes from placing an order to receiving the inventory, while demand variability pertains to the fluctuations in customer demand over time. By considering these factors, businesses can calculate the precise moment to reorder stock to maintain optimal inventory levels. The formula for calculating the reorder point typically includes the average daily demand, the lead time, and the safety stock, which serves as a buffer to account for uncertainties. This strategic approach helps businesses achieve a balance between maintaining sufficient inventory to meet customer demand and minimizing the costs associated with holding excess stock, ultimately enhancing overall supply chain efficiency and customer satisfaction.

6. Transportation Optimization: Transportation optimization is the strategic process of improving the efficiency, cost-effectiveness, and reliability of transporting goods within a supply chain. This involves determining the best routes, modes of transportation, and schedules to minimize costs, reduce transit times, and ensure timely deliveries. Key components of transportation optimization include route optimization, which uses advanced algorithms to identify the most efficient paths for delivery vehicles, and mode selection, which involves choosing the most appropriate transportation method (e.g., road, rail, air, sea) based on cost, speed, and the nature of the goods. Load optimization maximizes vehicle capacity utilization by efficiently loading goods, while dynamic routing adjusts routes in real-time based on changing conditions. Carrier selection involves evaluating and choosing the best carriers based on reliability and cost. By leveraging tracking technologies and sustainability initiatives, businesses can enhance visibility, reduce emissions, and achieve significant cost savings. Ultimately, transportation optimization ensures a streamlined, efficient, and responsive supply chain, leading to improved customer satisfaction and competitive advantage.

- **Route Optimization:** Route optimization is the process of planning the most efficient routes for transportation to minimize costs and delivery times. This involves using advanced algorithms and software to analyze various factors such as distance, traffic conditions, delivery windows, and vehicle capacity. By considering these elements, route optimization helps identify the best possible paths for delivery vehicles to follow, ensuring that goods are transported in the shortest time and at the lowest cost. This strategic approach not only reduces fuel consumption and operational expenses but also enhances customer satisfaction by ensuring timely deliveries. Route optimization can also improve overall fleet utilization, reduce wear and tear on vehicles, and contribute to environmental sustainability by lowering carbon emissions. By leveraging technology and data-driven insights, businesses can achieve significant improvements in their transportation operations, leading to a more efficient and responsive supply chain.
- **Mode Selection:** Mode selection refers to the process of choosing the most suitable mode of transportation, such as road, rail, air, or sea, based on several factors, including cost, speed, and distance. This strategic decision is crucial for optimizing logistics and supply chain operations.

Cost is a significant factor, as different modes of transportation have varying expense levels. For instance, sea freight is generally more cost-effective for large, bulky shipments over long distances, whereas air freight is more expensive but offers faster delivery times.

Speed is another critical consideration. Air transport is the fastest mode and is ideal for urgent or perishable goods, while road transport offers flexibility and convenience for short to medium distances. Rail transport provides a balance between cost and speed, suitable for heavy and bulk goods over long distances.

Distance plays a role in determining the most efficient mode of transportation. For example, sea transport is preferred for international shipments across continents, while road transport is optimal for local and regional deliveries.

By carefully evaluating these factors, businesses can select the most appropriate transportation mode to ensure timely, cost-effective, and efficient delivery of goods, ultimately enhancing overall supply chain performance.

7. Supplier Relationship Management: Supplier Relationship Management (SRM) is the strategic process of managing interactions and relationships with suppliers to maximize their value and performance. This involves evaluating, selecting, developing, and monitoring suppliers to ensure they align with the organization's goals and deliver consistent quality and reliability. Key aspects of SRM include assessing supplier capabilities, fostering collaboration and communication, managing risks, and continuously improving supplier performance through joint initiatives and shared best practices. Effective SRM enhances supply chain efficiency, reduces costs, improves product quality, and drives innovation, ultimately contributing to the organization's competitive advantage and sustainable growth.

- **Supplier Selection:** Supplier selection is the process of identifying and choosing suppliers based on key factors such as quality, cost, reliability, and capacity. This involves evaluating potential suppliers to ensure they meet the organization's standards and requirements. Quality is assessed to ensure the suppliers can consistently provide products or services that meet specifications. Cost evaluation focuses on finding suppliers that offer competitive pricing without compromising on quality. Reliability considers the suppliers' ability to deliver products on time and maintain consistent performance. Capacity evaluates the suppliers' ability to meet current and future demand. By carefully considering these factors, organizations can select suppliers that align with their strategic goals and contribute to an efficient and resilient supply chain.

- **Supplier Collaboration:** Supplier collaboration involves building strong, mutually beneficial relationships with suppliers to ensure the alignment of goals and improve overall supply chain performance. This collaborative approach focuses on open communication, trust, and joint problem-solving. By working closely with suppliers, businesses can share critical information, streamline processes, and innovate together. Effective supplier collaboration leads to enhanced efficiency, reduced costs, improved product quality, and faster response times to market changes. Additionally, it fosters a culture of continuous improvement, where both parties are committed to achieving common objectives and driving long-term success in the supply chain.

8. Tools and Technologies: Tools and technologies refer to the advanced systems, software, and devices used to enhance and streamline supply chain operations. These include Enterprise Resource Planning (ERP) systems, which integrate and manage core business processes; Transportation Management Systems (TMS), which optimize the planning and execution of transportation operations; and Warehouse Management Systems (WMS), which improve inventory control and warehouse efficiency. Additionally, technologies like the Internet of Things (IoT) enable real-time tracking and monitoring of goods, while artificial intelligence (AI) and machine learning algorithms enhance demand forecasting, route optimization, and decision-making. By leveraging these tools and technologies, businesses can achieve greater visibility, efficiency, and responsiveness in their supply chain operations, ultimately leading to improved performance and customer satisfaction.

9. Supply Chain Management Software: Supply Chain Management (SCM) software refers to a suite of integrated applications designed to manage, optimize, and streamline the various processes within a supply chain. These applications provide end-to-end visibility, control, and coordination of supply chain activities, including procurement, production, inventory management, transportation, and distribution. SCM software helps businesses improve efficiency, reduce costs, and enhance customer satisfaction by enabling real-time tracking and monitoring, advanced analytics, demand forecasting, and automated workflows. Key features often include supplier management, order processing, warehouse management, and transportation management. By leveraging SCM software, companies can achieve greater operational agility, better decision-making, and a more resilient and responsive supply chain.

- **ERP Systems:** Enterprise Resource Planning (ERP) systems, such as SAP and Oracle, are comprehensive software solutions designed to integrate and manage all aspects of supply chain operations within an organization. These systems provide a unified platform that consolidates various business processes, including procurement, production, inventory management, sales, and financial accounting. By offering real-time data visibility and seamless information flow across departments, ERP systems enable businesses to optimize resource allocation, improve operational efficiency, and enhance decision-making. The integration capabilities of ERP systems ensure that supply chain activities are coordinated and aligned with the organization's overall objectives, resulting in a more agile and responsive supply chain.
- **SCM Tools:** SCM tools refer to specialized supply chain management software like Kinaxis, JDA, and Llamasoft, designed for advanced planning and optimization. These tools provide robust capabilities for demand forecasting, inventory management, production planning, and transportation optimization. By leveraging advanced algorithms and analytics, SCM tools enable businesses to make data-driven decisions, enhance operational efficiency, and respond quickly to market changes. They offer real-time visibility into supply chain processes, facilitate collaboration among stakeholders, and help identify potential bottlenecks and opportunities for improvement. Overall, SCM tools are essential for achieving a more agile, responsive, and optimized supply chain.

10. Advanced Analytics: Advanced analytics refers to the application of sophisticated analytical techniques and tools to extract deeper insights, make data-driven decisions, and solve complex problems within an organization. This encompasses methods such as predictive analytics, which uses historical data and machine learning algorithms to forecast future trends and behaviors, and prescriptive analytics, which provides actionable recommendations based on data analysis. Advanced analytics also includes data mining, which involves discovering patterns and relationships in large datasets, and optimization techniques that enhance decision-making processes. By leveraging advanced analytics, businesses can improve operational efficiency, enhance customer experiences, and gain a competitive edge by uncovering hidden opportunities and mitigating potential risks.

- **Predictive Analytics:** Predictive analytics involves using data analytics to forecast future trends and inform decision-making processes. By analyzing historical data and employing advanced statistical techniques and machine learning algorithms, predictive analytics identifies patterns and relationships that can help anticipate future events and behaviors. This approach enables businesses to make proactive, data-driven decisions, optimize operations, and mitigate potential risks. Common applications of predictive analytics include demand forecasting, customer behavior analysis, risk assessment, and market trend prediction. By leveraging predictive analytics, organizations can enhance their strategic planning, improve operational efficiency, and gain a competitive advantage in the market.
- **Prescriptive Analytics:** Prescriptive analytics involves using data analysis to provide actionable recommendations that optimize supply chain performance. This advanced analytical approach combines historical data, real-time information, and predictive models to identify the best possible actions for achieving specific business goals. By evaluating various scenarios and potential outcomes, prescriptive analytics helps businesses make informed decisions that enhance efficiency, reduce costs, and improve overall supply chain effectiveness. This method not only predicts future trends but also suggests the optimal course of action to address potential issues and capitalize on opportunities, ensuring that supply chain operations are aligned with strategic objectives.

11. IoT and RFID: The Internet of Things (IoT) and Radio Frequency Identification (RFID) are technologies that enhance supply chain visibility and efficiency. IoT involves connecting physical devices to the internet, allowing them to collect and share data in real time. In supply chain management, IoT sensors can monitor the location, condition, and movement of goods, providing valuable insights for improving inventory management, tracking shipments, and ensuring product quality. RFID uses electromagnetic fields to automatically identify and track tags attached to objects. In supply chains, RFID tags can quickly and accurately track inventory levels, reduce manual scanning efforts, and improve accuracy in stock management. By leveraging IoT and RFID technologies, businesses can achieve greater transparency, reduce operational costs, and enhance overall supply chain performance.

- **IoT Devices:** IoT devices, or Internet of Things devices, are used to track and monitor goods throughout the supply chain, providing real-time visibility and enhancing operational efficiency. These devices are equipped with sensors that can collect data on the location, condition, and status of products as they move through various stages of the supply chain. By transmitting this data to centralized systems, IoT devices enable businesses to monitor inventory levels, track shipments, detect anomalies, and ensure product quality. This real-time visibility helps improve decision-making, optimize resource allocation, and enhance overall supply chain performance by reducing delays, minimizing losses, and improving customer satisfaction.
- **RFID Technology:** RFID technology, or Radio-Frequency Identification, involves the use of electromagnetic fields to automatically identify and track tags attached to objects, making it an efficient tool for inventory tracking and management. By implementing RFID technology, businesses can quickly and accurately monitor inventory levels, streamline stock-taking processes, and reduce manual scanning efforts. RFID tags store data electronically, which can be read by RFID readers without direct line-of-sight, allowing for faster and more efficient tracking of goods throughout the supply chain. This technology enhances inventory accuracy, reduces the likelihood of stockouts or overstocking, and improves overall operational efficiency. With RFID, businesses can achieve greater visibility and control over their inventory, leading to optimized supply chain performance and better customer satisfaction.

Conclusion:

Supply chain design and optimization are critical for developing efficient and resilient supply chains capable of adapting to evolving market conditions. By employing advanced techniques, strategies, and technologies, businesses can fine-tune their supply chain networks to enhance performance, reduce costs, and improve service levels. This involves a comprehensive approach to network design, inventory management, and supplier relationship management, as well as the use of cutting-edge tools and analytics. By strategically optimizing supply chain components, companies can achieve better coordination, faster response times, and greater operational agility, ultimately leading to increased customer satisfaction and competitive advantage in the market.

CHAPTER SEVENTEEN

ROLE OF IT AND AUTOMATION

Information Technology (IT) and automation have profoundly transformed industries such as supply chain management, manufacturing, and healthcare by enhancing efficiency, reducing costs, and improving overall performance. In supply chain management, IT and automation enable real-time tracking, advanced analytics, and seamless communication, leading to better decision-making and optimized operations. In manufacturing, automation streamlines production processes, increases precision, and reduces human error, resulting in higher productivity and quality. In healthcare, IT systems support electronic health records, telemedicine, and data-driven diagnostics, improving patient care and operational efficiency. By leveraging IT and automation, these industries can achieve greater scalability, innovation, and competitive advantage in an increasingly dynamic market. Here's a detailed look at their impact:

Role of IT: The role of Information Technology (IT) is pivotal in modern business and industrial landscapes, revolutionizing how organizations operate and compete. IT encompasses the use of computers, software, networks, and data management systems to streamline processes, enhance communication, and support decision-making. By leveraging IT, businesses can automate repetitive tasks, improve data accuracy, and ensure real-time access to critical information. This facilitates better coordination, efficient resource allocation, and faster response times. In industries such as supply chain management, manufacturing, and healthcare, IT enables advanced analytics, process optimization, and seamless integration of systems, leading to improved productivity, reduced costs, and enhanced service delivery. Overall, IT plays a critical role in driving innovation, efficiency, and competitive advantage in today's dynamic market environment.

1. **Data Management:** Data management is the systematic process of collecting, storing, organizing, and maintaining data to ensure its accuracy, accessibility, and security. It involves various activities such as data governance, data integration, data quality management, and data lifecycle management. Effective data management ensures that data is reliable, consistent, and available for decision-making and operational processes. By implementing robust data management practices, organizations can enhance data integrity, improve analytics, and support regulatory compliance. Ultimately, data management is essential for harnessing the full potential of data, enabling businesses to make informed decisions, drive innovation, and achieve strategic objectives.

- **Data Collection and Storage:** Data collection and storage refer to the capabilities of IT systems that allow for the gathering, storing, and managing of vast amounts of data. These systems facilitate the efficient accumulation of data from various sources, ensuring that it is organized and readily accessible. Collected data can be securely stored in databases and data warehouses, where it is maintained for future use. This data is invaluable for analysis, enabling businesses to derive insights, make informed decisions, and optimize processes. By leveraging IT systems for data collection and storage, organizations can enhance their operational efficiency, drive innovation, and improve overall business performance.
- **Data Security:** Data security involves implementing robust measures to protect sensitive information from cyber threats and unauthorized access. This encompasses a range of practices and technologies designed to ensure the confidentiality, integrity, and availability of data. Key components of data security include encryption, which secures data both in transit and at rest; access controls, which restrict data access to authorized personnel only; and regular security audits, which identify and address vulnerabilities. Additionally, businesses implement firewalls, intrusion detection systems, and multi-factor authentication to bolster their defenses against cyberattacks. By prioritizing data security, organizations can safeguard their sensitive information, maintain customer trust, and comply with regulatory requirements, ultimately enhancing their overall cybersecurity posture.

2. Communication and Collaboration: Communication and collaboration are essential components of modern business operations, facilitated significantly by Information Technology (IT). IT systems enable seamless communication across geographically dispersed teams through tools like email, instant messaging, video conferencing, and collaborative platforms. These technologies allow team members to share information, coordinate activities, and work together in real-time, regardless of their physical locations. Enhanced communication fosters a collaborative culture, improves decision-making, and accelerates problem-solving. Collaboration tools such as shared workspaces, document management systems, and project management software ensure that all team members have access to the latest information and can contribute effectively to projects. By leveraging IT for communication and collaboration, organizations can enhance productivity, streamline workflows, and foster innovation.

- **Enterprise Resource Planning (ERP):** Enterprise Resource Planning (ERP) systems are comprehensive software solutions that integrate various business functions, such as finance, human resources, and supply chain, into a single unified platform. By consolidating these diverse processes, ERP systems facilitate seamless communication and collaboration across departments, enabling organizations to operate more efficiently and effectively. The real-time data visibility provided by ERP systems ensures that all stakeholders have access to up-to-date information, promoting better decision-making and coordination. Additionally, ERP systems help streamline workflows, automate routine tasks, and improve data accuracy, leading to enhanced productivity and reduced operational costs. Overall, ERP systems play a crucial role in optimizing business operations and driving organizational success.
- **Collaboration Tools:** Collaboration tools like Microsoft Teams, Slack, and Zoom play a pivotal role in enabling real-time communication and collaboration among employees, regardless of their physical location. These tools offer various features such as instant messaging, video conferencing, file sharing, and project management capabilities, making it easy for team members to stay connected and work together efficiently. By facilitating seamless communication, these platforms help bridge the gap between remote and in-office workers, fostering a collaborative environment that enhances productivity and innovation. Additionally, collaboration tools support the integration of various

business applications, streamlining workflows and ensuring that all team members have access to the latest information and resources. Overall, these tools are essential for modern businesses to maintain effective communication, coordination, and collaboration in a distributed work environment.

3. Business Process Optimization: Business Process Optimization (BPO) refers to the strategic practice of streamlining and enhancing business processes to achieve greater efficiency, productivity, and effectiveness. This involves analyzing existing processes, identifying areas of improvement, and implementing changes to reduce waste, minimize errors, and accelerate workflows. By leveraging advanced technologies such as automation, artificial intelligence, and data analytics, organizations can optimize their operations, enhance customer experiences, and reduce operational costs. BPO focuses on continuous improvement, ensuring that processes remain agile and adaptable to changing market conditions and business needs. Ultimately, business process optimization enables organizations to achieve their strategic goals, drive innovation, and maintain a competitive edge in the market.

- **Customer Relationship Management (CRM):** Customer Relationship Management (CRM) systems are essential tools that help businesses manage customer interactions, track sales, and enhance customer service. By centralizing customer information and providing a comprehensive view of customer interactions, CRM systems enable businesses to better understand their customers' needs and preferences. These systems help track and analyze sales activities, manage leads, and monitor the progress of sales opportunities. Additionally, CRM systems support customer service teams by providing access to customer history and facilitating efficient resolution of inquiries and issues. By leveraging CRM systems, businesses can build stronger customer relationships, improve sales performance, and deliver personalized, high-quality customer service, ultimately driving customer satisfaction and loyalty.
- **Supply Chain Management (SCM):** Supply Chain Management (SCM) involves using IT systems to streamline supply chain operations, from procurement to distribution, by offering real-time visibility and tracking of goods. These systems enable businesses to monitor inventory levels, track shipments, and manage suppliers efficiently, ensuring that

products move smoothly through the supply chain. Real-time data and analytics facilitate informed decision-making, enhance coordination, and optimize resource allocation. By leveraging IT in SCM, organizations can reduce operational costs, improve product quality, and increase customer satisfaction, ultimately leading to a more resilient and responsive supply chain.

Role of Automation: Automation plays a crucial role in modern business operations by streamlining processes, reducing manual intervention, and enhancing overall efficiency. By implementing automated systems and technologies, organizations can perform repetitive tasks quickly and accurately, minimizing errors and freeing up employees to focus on more strategic activities. Automation optimizes workflows, accelerates production, and improves consistency in operations. In supply chain management, for instance, automation facilitates real-time tracking, inventory management, and demand forecasting, leading to a more responsive and resilient supply chain. In manufacturing, automation enhances precision and reduces production time, while in customer service, it enables prompt and accurate responses to inquiries. Ultimately, automation drives operational excellence, reduces costs, and supports scalability, enabling businesses to stay competitive in a dynamic market environment.

1. **Manufacturing:** In manufacturing, automation revolutionizes production processes by enhancing precision, efficiency, and consistency. Automated systems, such as robotic arms, assembly lines, and CNC machines, perform repetitive tasks with high accuracy, reducing human error and production time. These systems can work tirelessly around the clock, increasing output and productivity. Additionally, automation enables real-time monitoring and quality control, ensuring that products meet stringent standards. By integrating advanced technologies like IoT and AI, manufacturers can optimize workflows, predict maintenance needs, and respond swiftly to market demands. Overall, automation in manufacturing drives cost savings, improves product quality, and boosts operational agility, allowing companies to remain competitive in a rapidly evolving industry.

- **Industrial Robots:** Industrial robots are revolutionizing manufacturing processes by automating repetitive and hazardous tasks, thereby enhancing efficiency, precision, and safety. These robots, equipped with advanced sensors and programming, can perform tasks such as welding, assembly, packaging, and material handling with consistent accuracy and speed. By taking on labor-intensive and potentially dangerous activities, industrial robots reduce the risk of injuries to human workers and ensure a safer working environment. Additionally, their ability to operate continuously without fatigue leads to increased productivity and reduced production times. The precision of industrial robots also improves product quality and minimizes waste, making them an invaluable asset in modern manufacturing. Overall, the integration of industrial robots in manufacturing processes drives operational excellence, cost savings, and competitive advantage.

- **Automated Production Lines:** Automated production lines significantly enhance manufacturing processes by reducing the need for human intervention, increasing production speed, and ensuring consistent product quality. These lines utilize advanced machinery, robotics, and control systems to perform repetitive tasks with high precision and efficiency. By automating production, businesses can achieve higher output rates, minimize human errors, and maintain uniformity in their products. This consistency not only improves product reliability but also reduces waste and rework, leading to cost savings. Additionally, automated production lines can operate continuously, further boosting productivity and enabling manufacturers to meet market demands more effectively. Overall, the integration of automation in production lines drives operational excellence, improves scalability, and enhances competitiveness in the manufacturing industry.

2. Warehouse Management: Warehouse management involves the efficient oversight and control of warehouse operations to ensure the optimal storage, movement, and handling of goods. Automation in warehouse management plays a pivotal role in enhancing these operations by streamlining processes such as inventory tracking, order picking, and stock replenishment. Advanced technologies like automated storage and retrieval systems (AS/RS), robotic order pickers, and warehouse management software (WMS) facilitate real-time visibility and control over inventory levels, reduce labor costs, and minimize human errors. By implementing automated solutions, businesses can improve accuracy, speed up order fulfillment, and optimize space utilization within the warehouse. Overall, automation in warehouse management leads to increased productivity, cost savings, and better customer satisfaction by ensuring that goods are stored and dispatched efficiently.

- **Automated Storage and Retrieval Systems (AS/RS):** Automated Storage and Retrieval Systems (AS/RS) revolutionize warehouse operations by automating the storage and retrieval of goods, thereby increasing efficiency and reducing labor costs. These systems utilize advanced technology, including robotic cranes and conveyor systems, to handle goods with precision and speed. AS/RS can store and retrieve items from high-density storage racks, optimizing space utilization and ensuring quick access to inventory. By minimizing manual intervention, AS/RS reduces the likelihood of errors, enhances accuracy, and speeds up order fulfillment processes. This automation not only streamlines warehouse operations but also contributes to cost savings and improved productivity, ultimately enhancing overall supply chain performance.
- **Robotic Process Automation (RPA):** Robotic Process Automation (RPA) automates routine administrative tasks, such as inventory management and order processing, enhancing efficiency and allowing employees to focus on more strategic activities. By deploying software robots, RPA performs repetitive tasks quickly and accurately, minimizing human errors and reducing the workload on staff. These bots can handle a wide range of tasks, including data entry, invoice processing, and customer support, leading to improved operational efficiency and faster response times. RPA not only streamlines processes but also offers scalability, as the bots can handle increased volumes of work without additional resources. By freeing up employees from mundane tasks, RPA enables them to engage in higher-value activities that drive innovation and business growth.

3. Supply Chain and Logistics: Supply chain and logistics refer to the comprehensive management of the flow of goods, services, and information from the point of origin to the final destination. Automation and advanced technologies play a crucial role in optimizing these processes, enhancing efficiency, and reducing costs. Automated systems enable real-time tracking of shipments, inventory management, and demand forecasting, ensuring timely delivery and minimizing disruptions. Technologies such as IoT, RFID, and RPA facilitate seamless communication and coordination among different stakeholders, improving visibility and control over the entire supply chain. By leveraging these technologies, businesses can streamline operations, enhance customer satisfaction, and maintain a competitive edge in the market. Overall, automation in supply chain and logistics leads to increased productivity, reduced operational costs, and improved responsiveness to market demands.

- **Automated Guided Vehicles (AGVs):** Automated Guided Vehicles (AGVs) revolutionize warehouse and distribution center operations by automating the transportation of goods, thereby reducing the need for manual handling. These self-navigating vehicles use advanced sensors, navigation systems, and software to move pallets, containers, and other materials efficiently and accurately. AGVs can follow predefined paths or adjust routes dynamically based on real-time data, ensuring smooth and uninterrupted movement of goods. By automating this aspect of material handling, AGVs enhance productivity, reduce labor costs, and minimize the risk of injuries associated with manual lifting and transportation. Additionally, AGVs contribute to improved inventory management and faster order fulfillment, ultimately enhancing overall supply chain efficiency and responsiveness.
- **Route Optimization Software:** Route optimization software in logistics leverages automation to streamline and enhance delivery routes, resulting in reduced transportation costs and improved delivery times. This advanced software utilizes algorithms and real-time data to determine the most efficient routes for deliveries, taking into account factors such as traffic conditions, delivery windows, and vehicle capacities. By optimizing routes, the software minimizes unnecessary mileage and fuel consumption, leading to significant cost savings for logistics companies. Additionally, it ensures timely deliveries by avoiding delays and optimizing the sequence of stops, thereby enhancing customer satisfaction. Overall, route optimization software plays a crucial role in making logistics operations more efficient, cost-effective, and responsive to customer needs.

Benefits of IT and Automation: The benefits of Information Technology (IT) and automation are vast, transforming how businesses operate and compete in today's fast-paced environment. By integrating IT and automation, organizations can streamline processes, reduce operational costs, and enhance productivity. IT enables real-time data access and advanced analytics, facilitating informed decision-making and improving overall efficiency. Automation eliminates repetitive manual tasks, reduces errors, and accelerates workflows, allowing employees to focus on strategic activities. Together, IT and automation enhance customer experiences by enabling faster response times and personalized services. They also promote scalability and flexibility, allowing businesses to adapt to changing market demands. Ultimately, the adoption of IT and automation drives innovation, boosts competitiveness, and supports sustained growth.

1. Efficiency and Productivity: Efficiency and productivity are significantly enhanced through the integration of Information Technology (IT) and automation in business operations. By automating repetitive tasks and streamlining workflows, organizations can achieve faster and more accurate results, reducing the time and effort required for manual processes. IT systems provide real-time data access and analytics, enabling informed decision-making and quicker response times. Automation minimizes errors, ensures consistency, and increases output, allowing employees to focus on higher-value tasks. Overall, the adoption of IT and automation leads to optimized resource utilization, improved operational performance, and a more productive and efficient work environment.

- Automation significantly reduces the time and effort required for repetitive tasks, freeing employees to focus on higher-value activities. By deploying automated systems and tools, routine processes such as data entry, inventory management, and order processing can be executed swiftly and accurately with minimal human intervention. This not only increases operational efficiency but also reduces the risk of errors associated with manual handling. As a result, employees can dedicate more time and resources to strategic initiatives, creative problem-solving, and innovation, ultimately driving business growth and enhancing overall productivity. The shift from mundane tasks to more impactful work fosters a more engaged and motivated workforce, contributing to a dynamic and forward-thinking organizational culture.
- IT systems play a crucial role in streamlining business processes, thereby improving overall productivity and operational efficiency. These systems automate routine tasks, enhance data accuracy, and provide real-time access to critical information. By integrating various functions and facilitating seamless communication, IT systems ensure that workflows are optimized and resources are efficiently utilized. This reduces

bottlenecks and minimizes the time and effort required to complete tasks. Additionally, IT systems support advanced analytics, enabling data-driven decision-making and continuous process improvement. The result is a more agile and responsive organization capable of adapting to changing market demands and achieving higher levels of performance.

2. Cost Reduction: Cost reduction is a significant advantage of integrating Information Technology (IT) and automation into business operations. By automating repetitive and time-consuming tasks, businesses can minimize labor costs and reduce the need for extensive manual intervention. IT systems enable efficient resource management, streamline processes, and eliminate redundancies, leading to lower operational expenses. Additionally, automation improves accuracy and minimizes errors, reducing the costs associated with rework and corrections. Implementing advanced technologies such as predictive analytics and real-time monitoring helps organizations optimize inventory levels, reduce waste, and make more informed decisions. Overall, IT and automation contribute to substantial cost savings, allowing businesses to allocate resources more effectively and invest in strategic initiatives that drive growth and innovation.

- Automation significantly reduces labor costs by minimizing the need for manual intervention in repetitive tasks, which can be performed quickly and accurately by automated systems. This shift not only leads to lower labor expenses but also allows businesses to reallocate human resources to more strategic and high-value activities. Additionally, automation minimizes errors associated with manual processes, reducing the costs related to rework, corrections, and quality control. By streamlining operations and enhancing efficiency, automation contributes to significant cost savings, enabling organizations to optimize their budget allocation and invest in innovation and growth opportunities. Overall, the integration of automation in business processes drives substantial financial benefits, promoting a more cost-effective and productive operational environment.
- IT systems play a crucial role in enabling better resource management and reducing operational costs through data-driven decision-making. By leveraging advanced analytics and real-time data, IT systems provide valuable insights into resource utilization, inventory levels, and

operational performance. This allows businesses to make informed decisions, optimize resource allocation, and minimize waste. Automated processes and predictive analytics help identify inefficiencies and areas for improvement, ensuring that resources are used effectively and cost-effectively. Furthermore, IT systems facilitate proactive maintenance and asset management, reducing downtime and extending the lifespan of equipment. Overall, the integration of IT systems in resource management leads to enhanced efficiency, lower operational costs, and improved organizational performance.

3. Improved Accuracy and Quality: Improved accuracy and quality are paramount benefits of integrating Information Technology (IT) and automation into business processes. Automation minimizes human errors by handling repetitive tasks with precision and consistency, ensuring that outputs are accurate and reliable. IT systems provide real-time monitoring and advanced analytics, enabling businesses to identify and address quality issues promptly. By leveraging data-driven insights, organizations can implement quality control measures and continuously improve their processes. Additionally, IT and automation enhance standardization, ensuring that products and services meet established quality standards consistently. This focus on accuracy and quality not only boosts customer satisfaction but also reduces costs associated with rework and returns, ultimately driving business success and competitiveness.

- Automation plays a vital role in ensuring consistent and high-quality output by performing tasks with precision and uniformity, thereby reducing defects and the need for rework. Automated systems and machinery execute processes according to predefined standards, eliminating variability caused by human error. This results in products and services that consistently meet quality requirements. Additionally, automation enables continuous monitoring and quality control, promptly detecting and addressing any deviations from the desired outcomes. By maintaining a high level of accuracy and reliability, automation not only enhances product quality but also reduces waste and production costs, leading to more efficient and profitable operations.
- IT systems are instrumental in providing accurate and real-time data, which significantly enhances decision-making and overall business performance. By leveraging advanced data analytics and real-time

monitoring, IT systems enable organizations to gain valuable insights into their operations, market trends, and customer behaviors. This timely and precise information empowers businesses to make informed decisions quickly, respond to changing conditions, and seize new opportunities. Additionally, the accuracy of data provided by IT systems reduces the risk of errors, enhances efficiency, and supports strategic planning. Overall, the integration of IT systems into business operations leads to improved performance, increased competitiveness, and sustained growth.

Conclusion:

IT and automation are revolutionizing industries by significantly enhancing efficiency, reducing costs, and improving the quality of products and services. These technologies streamline operations, automate repetitive tasks, and provide real-time data and analytics, enabling businesses to make informed decisions quickly and accurately. As technology continues to advance, the integration of IT and automation will become even more vital in driving innovation and maintaining a competitive edge. Businesses that leverage these advancements will be better positioned to adapt to changing market demands, optimize their resources, and deliver superior value to their customers. Ultimately, the ongoing evolution of IT and automation will shape the future of industries, fostering a more efficient, agile, and innovative business landscape.

CHAPTER EIGHTEEN

DATA ANALYTICS AND INDUSTRIAL INTERNET OF THINGS (IIOT)

Data analytics involves examining raw data to draw conclusions and uncover patterns, trends, and insights that can help make informed decisions. Here are some key aspects: Descriptive analytics summarizes historical data to understand what has happened. Diagnostic analytics determines why certain events or trends occurred. Predictive analytics forecasts future outcomes based on historical data. Prescriptive analytics recommends actions to achieve desired outcomes. Real-time analytics processes and analyzes data as it is generated. Big data analytics analyzes large and complex datasets. Data quality and governance ensure data accuracy, consistency, and reliability. By leveraging these aspects, businesses can gain valuable insights, improve decision-making, and drive strategic initiatives. Here are some key aspects:

1. **Descriptive Analytics:** Descriptive analytics focuses on summarizing historical data to provide insights into what has happened. By using techniques such as data aggregation, data visualization, and statistical analysis, descriptive analytics transforms raw data into meaningful summaries and reports. This type of analysis helps organizations understand past trends, patterns, and performance metrics, enabling them to make data-driven decisions. Common tools for descriptive analytics include dashboards, charts, and graphs, which present data in an easily interpretable format. Overall, descriptive analytics serves as the foundation for more advanced analytics by providing a clear picture of past events and

establishing a baseline for future analysis.

- **Summary Statistics:** Summary statistics involve analyzing historical data to understand past events and trends. This type of analysis uses measures such as mean, median, mode, standard deviation, and variance to summarize and describe datasets. By examining these statistical metrics, organizations can gain insights into patterns, central tendencies, and data dispersion. Summary statistics provide a foundation for identifying historical performance, spotting trends, and making data-driven decisions. This analysis helps organizations understand what has happened in the past and establishes a baseline for future comparisons and deeper analysis.
- **Data Visualization:** Data visualization involves using tools like charts, graphs, and dashboards to present data insights in a visually appealing and comprehensible format. By transforming raw data into visual representations, data visualization helps uncover patterns, trends, and correlations that might be difficult to discern from raw data alone. Common types of visualizations include bar charts, line graphs, pie charts, scatter plots, and heatmaps. These visual tools make it easier for stakeholders to understand complex data, identify key insights, and make informed decisions. Effective data visualization enhances communication, facilitates data-driven decision-making, and provides a clear and intuitive way to explore and interpret data.

2. Predictive Analytics: Predictive analytics uses statistical models and machine learning algorithms to forecast future outcomes based on historical data. By analyzing past trends and patterns, predictive analytics helps organizations anticipate future events, such as customer behavior, market trends, and potential risks. This type of analysis enables businesses to make proactive decisions, optimize strategies, and allocate resources more effectively. Common applications of predictive analytics include demand forecasting, fraud detection, customer segmentation, and predictive maintenance. By leveraging predictive analytics, organizations can gain valuable insights, reduce uncertainty, and enhance their ability to achieve desired outcomes and stay competitive in the market.

- **Statistical Modeling:** Statistical modeling involves using techniques like regression analysis to predict future trends based on historical data.

Regression analysis identifies relationships between variables and quantifies how changes in one variable impact another. By analyzing historical data, statistical models can estimate future outcomes, helping organizations make informed decisions. These models are widely used in various fields, such as finance, marketing, and healthcare, for tasks like demand forecasting, risk assessment, and customer behavior prediction. Through statistical modeling, businesses gain valuable insights into future trends, enabling them to optimize strategies, allocate resources efficiently, and stay ahead in the competitive landscape.

- **Machine Learning:** Machine learning involves employing advanced algorithms to identify patterns within data and make predictions about future events. These algorithms analyze vast amounts of historical data, detecting trends and relationships that may not be immediately apparent to humans. By continuously learning from new data, machine learning models can refine their predictions and improve their accuracy over time. This technology is widely used in various applications, such as customer behavior forecasting, fraud detection, recommendation systems, and predictive maintenance. By leveraging machine learning, businesses can gain valuable insights, anticipate future outcomes, and make data-driven decisions that enhance their strategic planning and operational efficiency.

3. Prescriptive Analytics: Prescriptive analytics involves recommending specific actions to achieve desired outcomes based on data analysis and predictive modeling. This advanced form of analytics combines insights from descriptive and predictive analytics with optimization algorithms to suggest the best course of action. By analyzing multiple scenarios and considering various constraints, prescriptive analytics helps organizations make data-driven decisions that optimize performance, reduce risks, and maximize opportunities. Applications of prescriptive analytics include supply chain optimization, personalized marketing strategies, and resource allocation. By leveraging prescriptive analytics, businesses can navigate complex decision-making processes with greater confidence and achieve their strategic objectives more effectively.

- **Optimization:** Optimization in prescriptive analytics involves recommending the best course of action by analyzing various scenarios and potential outcomes. This process uses advanced algorithms to evaluate multiple variables and constraints, determining the most effective strategies to achieve desired objectives. By considering factors such as cost, resources, time, and risk, optimization helps organizations make data-driven decisions that maximize efficiency and performance. Applications of optimization include supply chain management, where it identifies the optimal inventory levels and distribution routes, and in marketing, where it suggests the most effective campaign strategies. Overall, optimization enables businesses to navigate complex decision-making processes with confidence, ensuring the best possible outcomes.

- **Decision Support Systems:** Decision Support Systems (DSS) utilize advanced analytics to provide actionable recommendations and assist organizations in making informed decisions. By integrating data from various sources and applying analytical models, DSS can evaluate multiple scenarios and predict potential outcomes. This enables businesses to identify the best strategies and solutions for complex problems. DSS tools often include interactive dashboards, simulation models, and optimization algorithms, which help decision-makers visualize data, explore alternatives, and assess risks. By leveraging these capabilities, Decision Support Systems enhance decision-making processes, improve operational efficiency, and contribute to achieving organizational goals more effectively.

Industrial Internet of Things (IIoT): The Industrial Internet of Things (IIoT) refers to the integration of connected devices, sensors, and advanced analytics in industrial settings to enhance operational efficiency, productivity, and overall performance. By leveraging IIoT technologies, industries can collect vast amounts of real-time data from machinery, equipment, and processes, enabling them to monitor, analyze, and optimize their operations.Here are some key components and benefits:

1. **Sensors and Actuators:** Sensors and actuators are integral components of the Industrial Internet of Things (IIoT), playing a crucial role in collecting data and executing actions. Sensors are devices that detect and measure physical properties such as temperature, pressure, humidity, and motion. They gather real-time data from machinery, equipment, and the environment, providing valuable insights into the operational conditions. Actuators, on the other hand, are devices that convert electrical signals into physical actions, such as opening a valve, adjusting a motor, or triggering an alarm. By working in tandem, sensors and actuators enable

automated monitoring, control, and optimization of industrial processes. This real-time feedback loop enhances efficiency, reduces downtime, and improves overall productivity in industrial settings.

- **Data Collection:** Sensors and actuators are integral components of the Industrial Internet of Things (IIoT), playing a crucial role in collecting data and executing actions. Sensors are devices that detect and measure physical properties such as temperature, pressure, humidity, and motion. They gather real-time data from machinery, equipment, and the environment, providing valuable insights into the operational conditions. Actuators, on the other hand, are devices that convert electrical signals into physical actions, such as opening a valve, adjusting a motor, or triggering an alarm. By working in tandem, sensors and actuators enable automated monitoring, control, and optimization of industrial processes. This real-time feedback loop enhances efficiency, reduces downtime, and improves overall productivity in industrial settings.
- **Control:** Actuators can adjust machine settings based on data analytics to optimize performance. By analyzing real-time data collected from sensors, advanced analytics can identify the optimal settings for machinery and equipment. Actuators then implement these adjustments automatically, ensuring that machines operate at peak efficiency. This dynamic control system enhances productivity, reduces energy consumption, and minimizes wear and tear on equipment. Additionally, actuators enable rapid response to changing conditions, maintaining consistent performance and preventing potential issues before they escalate. Overall, the integration of actuators with data analytics ensures a more efficient, reliable, and adaptive industrial operation.

2. Connectivity: Connectivity is a fundamental aspect of the Industrial Internet of Things (IIoT), enabling seamless communication between devices, sensors, and systems. Through advanced networking technologies, such as wireless communication, Ethernet, and IoT protocols, IIoT ensures that data is transmitted efficiently and reliably across the entire industrial environment. This interconnectedness allows for real-time data exchange, remote monitoring, and centralized control of operations. Enhanced connectivity facilitates the integration of various components, optimizing processes and improving decision-making. By ensuring that all devices and systems are connected and able to communicate, IIoT enhances overall operational efficiency, reduces downtime, and enables a more responsive and agile industrial ecosystem.

- **Network Infrastructure:** Network Infrastructure: Reliable and secure communication networks connect sensors, devices, and systems within the Industrial Internet of Things (IIoT). By leveraging advanced networking technologies, such as wireless communication, Ethernet, and IoT protocols, these networks ensure efficient and uninterrupted data transmission. Secure communication channels protect sensitive information from cyber threats, while robust infrastructure supports the scalability and reliability required for industrial operations. This interconnected network enables real-time data exchange, remote monitoring, and centralized control, optimizing processes and enhancing overall efficiency. Reliable network infrastructure is essential for maintaining seamless connectivity and ensuring the success of IIoT implementations in industrial environments.
- **Protocols:** Standardized communication protocols ensure interoperability between different devices and systems within the Industrial Internet of Things (IIoT). These protocols, such as MQTT, CoAP, and OPC UA, facilitate seamless communication and data exchange across diverse devices and platforms. By adhering to common standards, these protocols enable devices from different manufacturers to work together harmoniously, ensuring reliable and efficient operations. Standardized protocols also enhance scalability, allowing new devices and systems to be integrated into the existing network without compatibility issues. Overall, standardized communication protocols are essential for maintaining a cohesive and interoperable IIoT ecosystem, driving innovation and optimizing industrial processes.

3. Data Processing and Analysis: Data Processing and Analysis: In the Industrial Internet of Things (IIoT), data processing and analysis involve collecting, filtering, and interpreting vast amounts of real-time data generated by sensors and devices. Advanced analytics techniques, including machine learning and artificial intelligence, are used to extract valuable insights from this data. By processing and analyzing data, businesses can identify patterns, predict future trends, and make informed decisions. This helps optimize operations, improve efficiency, and enhance overall performance. Efficient data processing and analysis are essential for transforming raw data into actionable information, driving innovation, and maintaining a competitive edge in the industrial sector.

- **Edge Computing:** Edge Computing: Processing data near the source (at the edge) to reduce latency and bandwidth usage. By handling data closer to where it is generated, edge computing minimizes the time it takes to transfer data to central data centers, resulting in faster response times and improved real-time decision-making. Additionally, processing data at the edge reduces the amount of data that needs to be transmitted over networks, decreasing bandwidth usage and costs. This approach is particularly beneficial for applications requiring low latency and high reliability, such as industrial automation, autonomous vehicles, and smart cities. Overall, edge computing enhances efficiency and performance by bringing computation closer to the data source.
- **Cloud Computing:** Storing and analyzing large volumes of data in centralized data centers. This approach leverages powerful computing resources and scalable storage solutions to manage and process vast amounts of data. By utilizing cloud infrastructure, organizations can access advanced analytics tools, machine learning models, and data processing capabilities without the need for significant on-premises investments. Cloud computing enables remote access to data and applications, facilitating collaboration and flexibility. Additionally, centralized data centers offer robust security measures and disaster recovery options, ensuring data integrity and availability. Overall, cloud computing enhances efficiency, scalability, and innovation by providing a flexible and cost-effective platform for managing and analyzing large datasets.

Applications of Data Analytics and IIoT in Industrial Settings: Applications of Data Analytics and the Industrial Internet of Things (IIoT) in industrial settings are transforming operations by enhancing efficiency, productivity, and decision-making. Data analytics enables businesses to uncover insights from vast amounts of data, optimizing processes and predicting maintenance needs. IIoT connects sensors, devices, and systems, providing real-time monitoring and control of industrial operations. Together, they improve supply chain management, predictive maintenance, and quality control. For example, predictive maintenance uses data analytics and IIoT to anticipate equipment failures, reducing downtime and maintenance costs. In supply chain management, real-time tracking of inventory and assets enhances transparency and efficiency. Overall, these technologies drive innovation, competitiveness, and operational excellence in industrial environments.

1. **Predictive Maintenance:** Predictive maintenance uses advanced analytics and IIoT technologies to anticipate equipment failures and schedule maintenance activities before issues occur. By collecting and analyzing real-time data from sensors, predictive maintenance models can identify patterns and anomalies that indicate potential problems. This proactive approach minimizes unexpected downtime, extends the lifespan of machinery, and reduces maintenance costs. Industries benefit from improved operational efficiency, higher productivity, and enhanced reliability of their equipment. Predictive maintenance not only ensures that assets are maintained in optimal condition but also enables more effective resource allocation and strategic planning, ultimately contributing to a more resilient and efficient industrial operation.

- **Monitoring:** Continuous monitoring of equipment health to predict and prevent failures. By utilizing IIoT sensors and data analytics, businesses can continuously track the performance and condition of machinery in real-time. This constant vigilance allows for the early detection of anomalies and potential issues, enabling proactive maintenance interventions before failures occur. Continuous monitoring not only ensures the optimal performance of equipment but also minimizes unexpected downtime and maintenance costs. This approach enhances overall reliability and efficiency, contributing to smoother operations and higher productivity in industrial settings.
- **Scheduling:** Optimizing maintenance schedules based on data insights to reduce downtime and extend equipment life. By analyzing data from continuous equipment monitoring, businesses can identify the ideal times for maintenance activities, preventing unexpected breakdowns and minimizing disruption to operations. This data-driven approach allows for the efficient allocation of maintenance resources and ensures that machinery is serviced only when necessary, avoiding over- or under-maintenance. Optimized scheduling enhances equipment reliability, extends its lifespan, and reduces overall maintenance costs. Ultimately, leveraging data insights for maintenance scheduling

contributes to smoother, more efficient industrial operations and improved productivity.

2. Quality Control: Quality control ensures that products meet the desired standards and specifications by monitoring and inspecting production processes. Through data analytics and IIoT, businesses can collect real-time data on various quality parameters, such as dimensions, temperature, and pressure. By analyzing this data, organizations can identify deviations from the set standards and take corrective actions promptly. Automated quality control systems use sensors and machine learning algorithms to detect defects and anomalies, ensuring consistent product quality. This approach minimizes waste, reduces rework, and enhances customer satisfaction by delivering high-quality products. Overall, data-driven quality control improves efficiency, reduces costs, and maintains the reliability and reputation of the brand.

- **Real-Time Monitoring:** Real-Time Monitoring: Using sensors to detect defects and deviations in the production process. By employing IIoT sensors, businesses can continuously monitor various parameters such as temperature, pressure, and dimensions during production. This real-time data collection enables the immediate detection of anomalies and defects, allowing for prompt corrective actions. Automated systems analyze sensor data to identify deviations from predefined quality standards, ensuring consistent product quality. Real-time monitoring helps minimize waste, reduce rework, and enhance overall efficiency by maintaining high-quality standards throughout the production process. Ultimately, this approach leads to better product quality, increased customer satisfaction, and improved operational performance.
- **Analytics:** Analyzing data to identify root causes of quality issues and implement corrective actions. By leveraging advanced data analytics techniques, businesses can examine historical and real-time data to pinpoint the underlying causes of quality problems. This involves identifying patterns, correlations, and anomalies that indicate deviations from the desired standards. Root cause analysis enables organizations to understand why defects or issues occur and to develop targeted solutions to address them. By implementing corrective actions based on data-driven insights, businesses can prevent recurring quality problems, improve product consistency, and enhance overall production

efficiency. This proactive approach ensures higher quality products, reduces waste, and strengthens customer satisfaction.

3. Energy Management: Energy Management: Optimizing the consumption and utilization of energy resources to improve efficiency and reduce costs. By leveraging data analytics and IIoT technologies, businesses can monitor energy usage in real-time, identify inefficiencies, and implement energy-saving measures. Smart sensors and meters collect data on energy consumption patterns, enabling organizations to detect areas of waste and opportunities for improvement. Advanced analytics provide insights into peak usage times, equipment performance, and energy-saving strategies. By optimizing energy management, industries can reduce operational costs, lower their carbon footprint, and enhance overall sustainability. This proactive approach ensures efficient energy utilization and supports environmental responsibility in industrial settings.

- **Energy Consumption Monitoring:** Energy Consumption Monitoring: Tracking energy usage in real-time to identify inefficiencies. By using smart sensors and meters, businesses can continuously monitor energy consumption across various operations and equipment. This real-time tracking provides detailed insights into usage patterns, peak demand periods, and potential areas of waste. Advanced analytics can then process this data to identify inefficiencies, such as excessive energy usage during non-peak hours or suboptimal equipment performance. By pinpointing these issues, organizations can implement energy-saving measures, optimize processes, and reduce operational costs. Overall, real-time energy consumption monitoring enhances efficiency, promotes sustainable practices, and supports effective energy management strategies.
- **Optimization:** Implementing strategies to reduce energy consumption and costs. By analyzing real-time energy usage data, businesses can identify inefficiencies and develop targeted measures to optimize energy consumption. This may involve upgrading equipment to more energy-efficient models, implementing automated control systems to adjust energy use based on demand, and optimizing production schedules to minimize energy-intensive operations during peak hours. Additionally, incorporating renewable energy sources and energy recovery systems can further reduce dependency on traditional energy sources. By

adopting these optimization strategies, organizations can achieve significant cost savings, enhance sustainability, and improve overall operational efficiency.

4. Supply Chain Optimization: Enhancing the efficiency and effectiveness of the supply chain through data analytics and IIoT technologies. By collecting real-time data from various points in the supply chain, such as inventory levels, transportation routes, and demand patterns, businesses can gain valuable insights into their operations. Advanced analytics and machine learning algorithms can analyze this data to identify bottlenecks, optimize routes, and forecast demand. This proactive approach enables better inventory management, reduced lead times, and improved customer satisfaction. Overall, supply chain optimization ensures a smoother flow of goods, minimizes costs, and enhances the agility and responsiveness of the entire supply chain network.

- **Inventory Management:** Inventory management leverages data analytics to effectively forecast demand and optimize inventory levels. By analyzing historical sales data, market trends, and customer behavior, businesses can predict future demand with greater accuracy, thus minimizing overstock and stockouts. Advanced analytics tools allow for real-time monitoring of inventory levels, enabling timely restocking and efficient allocation of resources. This data-driven approach not only enhances operational efficiency but also reduces costs, increases customer satisfaction, and strengthens the overall supply chain strategy.
- **Logistics:** Logistics can significantly enhance transportation and distribution efficiency through the use of real-time tracking and route optimization. By employing GPS technology and advanced analytics, companies can monitor the precise location of their vehicles, allowing for more accurate delivery times and quicker response to any disruptions. Route optimization algorithms analyze traffic patterns, road conditions, and delivery schedules to determine the most efficient paths, reducing fuel consumption and transit times. This approach not only cuts operational costs but also improves customer satisfaction by ensuring timely and reliable deliveries, ultimately strengthening the overall logistics network.

Benefits:

- **Improved Efficiency:** Improved efficiency through automation and data-driven insights leads to optimized processes and reduced waste. By implementing automated systems, businesses can streamline repetitive tasks, freeing up human resources for more strategic activities. Data-driven insights enable better decision-making by identifying inefficiencies and opportunities for improvement. This dual approach minimizes errors, reduces resource consumption, and enhances productivity. Consequently, organizations can achieve cost savings, improve service quality, and contribute to sustainable practices by minimizing waste and environmental impact.
- **Cost Savings:** Predictive maintenance and energy management play a crucial role in reducing operational costs. By using advanced analytics and IoT sensors, businesses can monitor equipment performance and identify potential issues before they lead to costly breakdowns. This proactive approach minimizes downtime and extends the lifespan of assets. Additionally, energy management systems optimize energy consumption by tracking usage patterns and implementing energy-saving measures. Together, these strategies result in significant cost savings, improved efficiency, and a more sustainable operation.
- **Enhanced Decision-Making:** Enhanced decision-making is driven by the power of real-time data and advanced analytics, enabling organizations to make better and faster decisions. Access to up-to-the-minute information allows for a more accurate assessment of current conditions, while advanced analytics provide deep insights by identifying patterns and trends. This combination of timely data and sophisticated analysis empowers businesses to respond swiftly to changing circumstances, seize opportunities, and mitigate risks more effectively. Ultimately, it leads to more informed, strategic, and agile decision-making processes.
- **Increased Safety:** Increased safety in the workplace can be achieved through monitoring and analytics, which help identify potential hazards before they cause harm. By employing real-time sensors and data analysis, organizations can detect unsafe conditions, equipment malfunctions, or risky behaviors. This proactive approach enables timely interventions, such as maintenance, training, or process adjustments, to prevent accidents and injuries. Ultimately, leveraging monitoring and analytics for safety not only protects employees but also fosters a culture of continuous improvement and accountability.

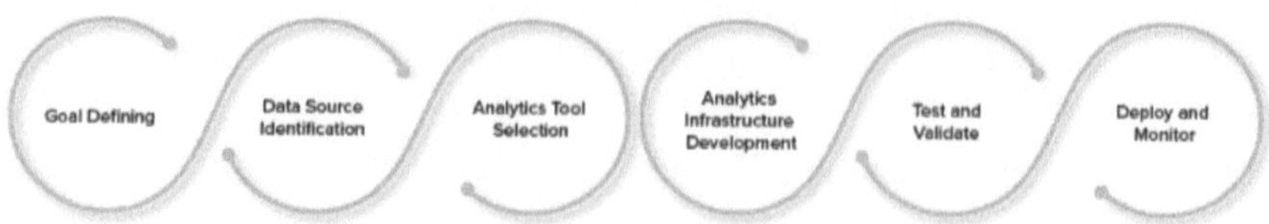

IoT Analytics

Conclusion:

Data analytics and the Industrial Internet of Things (IIoT) are revolutionizing industries by delivering valuable insights, enhancing efficiency, and enabling automation. By harnessing data from interconnected devices and advanced analytics, businesses can gain a deeper understanding of their operations, identify areas for improvement, and optimize processes. This integration leads to increased productivity, reduced costs, and better decision-making. As technology continues to evolve, the synergy between data analytics and IIoT will become even more critical in driving innovation and maintaining competitiveness in industrial environments.

CHAPTER NINETEEN

Real-World Applications in Different Industries

Manufacturing has undergone a transformation driven by technology, resulting in increased efficiency and innovation. Automation, data analytics, and the Industrial Internet of Things (IIoT) have revolutionized production processes by enabling real-time monitoring, predictive maintenance, and smart manufacturing. These advancements allow for greater precision, reduced downtime, and optimized resource utilization. As technology continues to evolve, the manufacturing sector will further benefit from the integration of artificial intelligence, machine learning, and robotics, ultimately leading to higher productivity, improved quality, and enhanced competitiveness in the global market. Manufacturing is the process of transforming raw materials into finished products through the use of machinery, tools, labor, and technology. It serves as the backbone of industrial economies, enabling the mass production of goods that meet consumer and market demands. Modern manufacturing incorporates advanced techniques such as automation, robotics, and digital technologies to enhance efficiency, precision, and scalability. Additionally, sustainable practices, including energy efficiency, waste reduction, and the use of renewable resources, are increasingly becoming integral to manufacturing. This vital sector drives economic growth, supports innovation, and plays a critical role in improving the quality of life by delivering essential products to societies worldwide.

1. Predictive Maintenance: Predictive maintenance leverages advanced analytics and IoT sensors to monitor the condition of equipment and predict potential failures before they occur. By continuously collecting and analyzing data on machinery performance, businesses can identify patterns and anomalies that signal imminent issues. This proactive approach allows for timely maintenance, minimizing unexpected downtime, and extending the lifespan of assets. Ultimately, predictive maintenance enhances operational efficiency, reduces maintenance costs, and improves overall productivity.

- **Application:** Application of sensors in machinery involves collecting data on temperature, vibration, and other parameters to monitor equipment health and performance. These sensors continuously gather real-time information, which is then analyzed to identify patterns and anomalies. By detecting early signs of potential issues, businesses can take preventive measures to avoid equipment failures and downtime. This data-driven approach enhances predictive maintenance, optimizes operational efficiency, and extends the lifespan of machinery, ultimately leading to cost savings and improved productivity.
- **Impact:** Analyzing data collected from machinery sensors predicts potential equipment failures, enabling proactive maintenance and significantly reducing downtime. By identifying patterns and anomalies in parameters like temperature and vibration, businesses can address issues before they escalate into costly breakdowns. This data-driven approach not only ensures continuous operation and minimizes disruptions but also extends the lifespan of equipment, leading to overall cost savings and enhanced productivity.

2. Quality Control: Quality control in manufacturing ensures that products meet specified standards and requirements. By implementing rigorous testing procedures and monitoring key metrics throughout the production process, businesses can identify defects and inconsistencies early on. Advanced technologies, such as automated inspection systems and data analytics, enhance the accuracy and efficiency of quality control. This proactive approach not only reduces waste and rework but also improves product reliability and customer satisfaction, ultimately contributing to a stronger reputation and competitive advantage in the market. Quality control is a systematic process aimed at ensuring that products and services meet established standards of quality and reliability. It involves monitoring and testing various aspects of production, from raw materials to finished goods, to identify and address deviations from required specifications. Techniques such as inspections, statistical analysis, and automated testing are commonly employed to maintain consistency and prevent defects. Quality control not only enhances customer satisfaction by delivering dependable products but also reduces waste and operational costs by improving efficiency. As a critical element of manufacturing, quality control supports brand reputation, regulatory compliance, and long-term business success.

- **Application:** Application of sensors and analytics in monitoring production processes involves real-time data collection and analysis to ensure optimal performance and quality. Sensors are installed on machinery and throughout production lines to continuously measure parameters such as temperature, pressure, and speed. The collected data is then analyzed using advanced analytics to detect deviations, identify inefficiencies, and predict potential issues. This real-time monitoring enables immediate corrective actions, ensuring consistent product quality, reducing waste, and enhancing overall efficiency in manufacturing operations.
- **Impact:** Detecting defects early and ensuring consistent product quality has a significant impact on manufacturing operations. By leveraging real-time monitoring and analytics, businesses can promptly identify and address issues, ensuring that products meet quality standards from the outset. This proactive approach minimizes waste and reduces the need for costly rework, ultimately leading to lower production costs and higher efficiency. Additionally, maintaining consistent product quality enhances customer satisfaction and strengthens the brand's reputation in the market.

Healthcare is experiencing a significant transformation through technological advancements and innovative practices. The integration of data analytics, telemedicine, and wearable health devices is revolutionizing patient care. Real-time data monitoring enables early diagnosis and personalized treatment plans, improving overall health outcomes. Telemedicine provides convenient access to medical consultations, reducing the need for in-person visits and enhancing healthcare accessibility. Additionally, AI-powered systems assist in medical research and administrative tasks, increasing efficiency and accuracy. As technology continues to evolve, the healthcare sector will further benefit from these innovations, leading to better patient care and more sustainable practices.

1. Remote Patient Monitoring: Remote patient monitoring (RPM) allows healthcare providers to track patients' vital signs and health data in real time from a distance. Utilizing wearable devices and smart sensors, RPM collects information such as heart rate, blood pressure, and glucose levels, transmitting this data to healthcare professionals. This continuous monitoring enables early detection of potential health issues, timely interventions, and personalized care plans. RPM improves patient outcomes, reduces hospital visits, and enhances the overall efficiency of healthcare delivery, making it a vital component in modern healthcare systems.

- **Application:** Wearable devices collect patient data, such as heart rate, glucose levels, and physical activity, and transmit this information to healthcare providers in real time. These devices, including smartwatches and continuous glucose monitors, enable continuous monitoring of patients' vital signs and health metrics. The collected data is analyzed to detect any abnormalities or trends, allowing for early intervention and personalized treatment plans. This application of wearable technology improves patient outcomes, enhances preventive care, and reduces the need for frequent in-person visits, making healthcare more efficient and accessible.
- **Impact:** Real-time monitoring through wearable devices significantly impacts patient care by enabling early intervention and timely responses to health issues. By continuously tracking vital signs and health metrics, healthcare providers can detect abnormalities and trends promptly, allowing for personalized and preventive treatment plans. This proactive approach improves patient outcomes by addressing potential problems before they escalate, reducing the need for hospital visits and admissions. Ultimately, real-time monitoring enhances the efficiency and effectiveness of healthcare delivery, leading to better overall patient health and well-being.

2. Hospital Resource Management: Hospital resource management involves efficiently allocating and utilizing resources such as staff, equipment, and facilities to ensure optimal patient care. By leveraging advanced analytics and real-time data, hospitals can monitor resource usage, predict demand, and adjust allocations accordingly. This proactive approach helps to reduce wait times, prevent resource shortages, and enhance overall operational efficiency. Effective resource management not only improves patient outcomes but also maximizes the productivity and cost-effectiveness of healthcare institutions, ultimately contributing to a higher standard of care.

- **Application:** Analyzing patient flow and resource utilization data involves collecting and examining information on the movement of patients through various hospital departments and the usage of resources like staff, beds, and equipment. By leveraging advanced analytics, hospitals can identify bottlenecks, predict peak times, and optimize resource allocation to ensure efficient operations. This data-driven approach enables better scheduling, reduces wait times, and improves the overall patient experience. Effective analysis of patient flow and resource utilization data ultimately enhances hospital efficiency, leading to higher quality care and improved patient outcomes.
- **Impact:** Optimizing staff allocation, reducing wait times, and improving overall efficiency have a profound impact on hospital operations. By analyzing patient flow and resource utilization data, hospitals can better allocate staff to match patient demand, ensuring that the right personnel are available when needed. This proactive approach minimizes bottlenecks and shortens patient wait times, leading to a more streamlined and efficient healthcare delivery process. Ultimately, these improvements enhance patient satisfaction, reduce operational costs, and elevate the overall quality of care provided.

Transportation and Logistics have evolved significantly with the integration of advanced technologies, enhancing efficiency and reliability. Real-time tracking systems enable precise monitoring of shipments, providing transparency and reducing delays. Route optimization algorithms analyze traffic and road conditions to determine the most efficient paths, minimizing fuel consumption and transit times. Additionally, automated warehouses and robotic systems streamline sorting and handling processes, improving overall productivity. These innovations not only reduce operational costs but also enhance customer satisfaction by ensuring timely and accurate deliveries, making transportation and logistics more efficient and effective.

1. Fleet Management: Fleet management involves the efficient administration and coordination of a company's vehicle fleet to ensure optimal performance and cost-effectiveness. Utilizing GPS tracking, telematics, and data analytics, businesses can monitor vehicle locations, driver behavior, and maintenance needs in real time. This proactive approach allows for better route planning, fuel management, and timely maintenance, reducing downtime and operational costs. Effective fleet management enhances productivity, improves safety, and ensures that vehicles are utilized to their full potential, ultimately leading to a more efficient and reliable transportation system.

- **Application:** Telematics systems are employed to gather comprehensive data on vehicle location, speed, and fuel consumption. These systems use GPS technology and onboard sensors to track real-time movements and performance metrics of each vehicle in the fleet. The collected data is then analyzed to optimize route planning, monitor driver behavior, and enhance fuel efficiency. This application of telematics enables businesses to improve fleet management, reduce operational costs, and ensure timely maintenance, ultimately leading to a more efficient and sustainable transportation system.
- **Impact:** Optimizing routes through telematics systems has a substantial impact on transportation efficiency. By analyzing real-time data on vehicle location, speed, and traffic conditions, businesses can determine the most efficient paths for their fleets. This strategic route planning reduces fuel consumption and operational costs while improving delivery times. Enhanced route optimization not only leads to significant cost savings but also ensures timely and reliable deliveries, ultimately boosting customer satisfaction and overall fleet productivity.

2. Warehouse Automation: Warehouse automation involves the use of advanced technologies such as robotics, conveyor systems, and automated storage and retrieval systems (AS/RS) to streamline and optimize warehouse operations. These technologies enable efficient handling, sorting, and storage of goods, reducing manual labor and minimizing errors. Automation enhances inventory accuracy, speeds up order fulfillment, and improves overall productivity. By integrating warehouse management systems (WMS) with automation solutions, businesses can achieve seamless coordination and real-time visibility of inventory, leading to cost savings, increased efficiency, and enhanced customer satisfaction.

- **Application:** Automated guided vehicles (AGVs) and robotic systems are revolutionizing inventory management and order fulfillment processes. AGVs navigate warehouse floors autonomously, transporting goods to their designated locations with precision and efficiency. Robotic systems, including robotic arms and conveyors, handle tasks such as sorting, picking, and packing items. These automation technologies streamline operations, reduce manual labor, and minimize errors, leading to faster order processing and improved accuracy. The integration of AGVs and robotics enhances overall warehouse productivity, ensuring timely and reliable deliveries while optimizing resource utilization.
- **Impact:** The impact of warehouse automation, including automated guided vehicles (AGVs) and robotic systems, is significant in increasing efficiency, reducing labor costs, and minimizing errors in warehouse operations. By automating tasks such as inventory management, order fulfillment, and goods transportation, businesses can streamline processes and enhance productivity. Automation reduces reliance on manual labor, leading to cost savings and a decrease in human error. This results in faster order processing, improved accuracy, and overall operational efficiency, ultimately contributing to better customer satisfaction and competitive advantage in the market.

Energy and Utilities The energy and utilities sector is undergoing significant transformation driven by technological advancements and increasing focus on sustainability. Integrating smart grids, renewable energy sources, and advanced data analytics is revolutionizing the way energy is produced, distributed, and consumed. Smart grids enhance reliability and efficiency by enabling real-time monitoring and automated management of energy flows. The adoption of renewable energy sources, such as solar and wind, reduces dependency on fossil fuels and lowers carbon emissions. Advanced data analytics provide insights into energy usage patterns, facilitating better demand forecasting and optimizing resource allocation. These innovations are paving the way for a more sustainable and resilient energy future, ensuring reliable and efficient energy delivery while minimizing environmental impact.

1. Smart Grid Management: Smart grid management leverages advanced technologies to enhance the efficiency, reliability, and sustainability of electricity distribution. By integrating sensors, smart meters, and data analytics, smart grids enable real-time monitoring and automated control of energy flows. This allows for better demand response, reduced energy losses, and improved integration of renewable energy sources. Smart grid management also enhances fault detection and quickens response times, minimizing outages and ensuring a more resilient energy infrastructure. Ultimately, smart grids contribute to a more efficient and sustainable energy system that benefits both utilities and consumers.

- **Application:** Sensors and smart meters are utilized to collect real-time data on energy usage and grid performance. These devices monitor various parameters, such as electricity consumption, voltage levels, and grid stability, providing valuable insights into the efficiency and reliability of the energy system. The collected data is analyzed to detect anomalies, optimize energy distribution, and enhance demand response strategies. This application of advanced monitoring technology enables utilities to improve grid management, reduce energy losses, and ensure a more resilient and efficient energy infrastructure.
- **Impact:** Improving energy distribution, detecting faults quickly, and reducing energy waste have significant impacts on the energy and utilities sector. By leveraging smart grid technology, real-time data from sensors and smart meters enables precise monitoring and control of energy flows. This ensures that energy is distributed efficiently, reducing losses and enhancing reliability. Rapid fault detection minimizes outages and allows for prompt corrective actions, ensuring a stable energy supply. Overall, these advancements contribute to a more efficient, sustainable, and resilient energy system, benefiting both utilities and consumers.

2. Renewable Energy Optimization: Renewable energy optimization focuses on maximizing the efficiency and effectiveness of renewable energy sources like solar, wind, and hydroelectric power. By leveraging advanced technologies and data analytics, energy producers can monitor and manage the performance of renewable energy systems in real time. This involves analyzing weather patterns, energy output, and grid integration to ensure optimal energy production and distribution. Enhancing renewable energy optimization reduces dependency on fossil fuels, lowers carbon emissions, and promotes a sustainable energy future, ultimately contributing to environmental conservation and energy security.

- **Application:** Using data analytics to predict weather patterns and optimize renewable energy sources involves collecting and analyzing meteorological data to forecast conditions like sunlight, wind speeds, and precipitation. This information helps energy producers determine the optimal times for harnessing solar, wind, and hydroelectric power. By accurately predicting weather patterns, they can adjust the operation of renewable energy systems to maximize efficiency and output. This application enhances the reliability and effectiveness of renewable energy, reduces reliance on fossil fuels, and supports a more sustainable energy future.
- **Impact:** Maximizing energy production from wind, solar, and other renewable sources has a profound impact on reducing reliance on fossil fuels. By leveraging advanced data analytics and real-time monitoring, renewable energy systems can operate at peak efficiency, harnessing the maximum potential of natural resources. This optimized energy production decreases the need for fossil fuel-based power generation, leading to lower carbon emissions and a cleaner environment. Additionally, the increased use of renewable energy sources enhances energy security and sustainability, contributing to a more resilient and eco-friendly energy infrastructure.

Agriculture is experiencing a revolution with the adoption of advanced technologies, improving efficiency and sustainability. Precision farming uses GPS and data analytics to optimize planting, irrigation, and harvesting, ensuring better crop yields and resource management. Drones and sensors monitor crop health and soil conditions in real time, enabling timely interventions. Additionally, automated machinery reduces manual labor and enhances productivity. These innovations lead to higher crop quality, reduced environmental impact, and increased profitability for farmers, ultimately contributing to global food security and sustainable agricultural practices.

1. Precision Farming: Precision farming utilizes advanced technologies such as GPS, sensors, and data analytics to optimize agricultural practices.

By precisely monitoring and managing variables like soil conditions, moisture levels, and crop health, farmers can make informed decisions to enhance productivity and resource efficiency. This method allows for targeted application of water, fertilizers, and pesticides, reducing waste and environmental impact. Precision farming increases crop yields, improves quality, and promotes sustainable agriculture by ensuring that resources are used efficiently and effectively throughout the farming process.

- **Application:** Sensors monitor soil moisture, crop health, and weather conditions to provide real-time data for precision farming. These sensors collect vital information on factors such as humidity, temperature, and nutrient levels in the soil, as well as the overall health of crops. By analyzing this data, farmers can make informed decisions about irrigation, fertilization, and pest control, ensuring optimal growing conditions. This application of sensor technology enhances crop yields, reduces resource waste, and promotes sustainable agricultural practices by enabling more efficient and effective farm management.
- **Impact:** Optimizing irrigation, fertilization, and pesticide use through precision farming significantly impacts agricultural productivity and sustainability. By precisely monitoring soil moisture, crop health, and weather conditions, farmers can apply water, nutrients, and pesticides only when and where needed, reducing waste and environmental impact. This targeted approach increases crop yields and enhances the quality of produce. Additionally, efficient resource utilization leads to cost savings and promotes more sustainable farming practices, ultimately contributing to improved food security and environmental conservation.

2. Livestock Monitoring: Livestock monitoring involves using advanced technologies such as GPS, sensors, and wearable devices to track the health, behavior, and location of animals. These tools provide real-time data on vital signs, movement patterns, and feeding habits, enabling farmers to promptly address any health issues and optimize animal welfare. By monitoring environmental conditions and resource usage, livestock monitoring helps improve efficiency and productivity in farming operations. This technology enhances animal health management, reduces labor costs, and ensures sustainable and ethical livestock practices, ultimately contributing to better farm profitability and food security.

- **Application:** Wearable devices are used to track the health and behavior of livestock, providing real-time data on vital signs, activity levels, and movement patterns. These devices, such as smart collars and ear tags, monitor factors like heart rate, body temperature, and location. By analyzing this data, farmers can detect early signs of illness, optimize feeding schedules, and ensure proper animal welfare. This application of wearable technology enhances livestock management, improves productivity, and promotes sustainable and ethical farming practices by enabling timely and informed decision-making.
- **Impact:** Early detection of diseases, improving animal welfare, and optimizing breeding and feeding practices have a significant impact on livestock management. Wearable devices provide real-time data on animals' health and behavior, enabling farmers to identify and address health issues promptly. This proactive approach enhances animal welfare by ensuring timely medical intervention and proper care. Additionally, analyzing data on feeding and breeding patterns allows for optimized practices, leading to better productivity and efficiency. Ultimately, these advancements contribute to healthier livestock, increased farm profitability, and more sustainable and ethical farming practices.

Retail industry is rapidly evolving with the integration of advanced technologies and changing consumer preferences. Digital transformation, including e-commerce and mobile shopping, has reshaped the way customers shop, offering convenience and personalized experiences. In-store technologies such as self-checkout systems, augmented reality, and smart shelves enhance the shopping experience by providing real-time information and interactive features. Additionally, data analytics and artificial intelligence enable retailers to understand customer behavior, optimize inventory management, and tailor marketing strategies. These innovations lead to improved customer satisfaction, operational efficiency, and competitive advantage in the retail market.

1. Inventory Management: Inventory management in retail involves tracking and controlling stock levels to ensure products are available to meet customer demand while minimizing excess inventory. Advanced technologies like RFID tags, barcode scanning, and inventory management software provide real-time visibility into stock levels and locations. These tools enable retailers to optimize inventory turnover, reduce stockouts, and prevent overstock situations. Effective inventory management ensures that the right products are available at the right time, enhancing customer satisfaction and improving operational efficiency. By accurately forecasting demand and managing stock levels, retailers can reduce costs, improve profitability, and maintain a competitive edge.

- **Application:** RFID tags and sensors are utilized to track inventory levels in real time, providing accurate and up-to-date information on stock availability. These technologies enable automated data collection by scanning RFID tags on products as they move through the supply chain and retail environment. By continuously monitoring inventory, retailers can quickly identify stockouts, prevent overstock situations, and optimize replenishment processes. This real-time visibility enhances inventory management, reduces operational costs, and ensures that customers have access to the products they need when they need them, ultimately improving overall customer satisfaction and operational efficiency.
- **Impact:** Reducing stockouts and overstock situations through technologies like RFID tags and sensors significantly improves supply chain efficiency and enhances customer satisfaction. Real-time tracking of inventory levels enables retailers to maintain optimal stock levels, ensuring that products are always available when customers need them while minimizing excess inventory. This efficient inventory management reduces operational costs associated with storage and unsold goods. By preventing stockouts, retailers can avoid missed sales opportunities, and by avoiding overstock, they can reduce waste and markdowns. Overall, these improvements lead to a more reliable supply chain, better customer experiences, and increased profitability for retailers.

2. Personalized Shopping Experiences: Personalized shopping experiences leverage customer data and advanced technologies to tailor the retail journey to individual preferences. By analyzing purchase history, browsing behavior, and demographic information, retailers can offer customized product recommendations, targeted promotions, and personalized marketing messages. In-store technologies such as augmented reality and interactive displays further enhance the shopping experience by providing tailored information and engaging features. Personalized shopping experiences not only increase customer satisfaction and loyalty but also drive sales by offering relevant and appealing options, making the retail journey more enjoyable and efficient for each customer.

- **Application:** Analyzing customer data allows retailers to recommend products and create personalized offers tailored to individual preferences. By examining purchase history, browsing behavior, and demographic information, retailers can identify patterns and predict customer needs. This data-driven approach enables the creation of customized product recommendations, targeted promotions, and exclusive offers that resonate with each customer. The application of customer data analysis enhances the shopping experience by making it more relevant and engaging, ultimately increasing customer satisfaction, loyalty, and sales.
- **Impact:** Increasing customer engagement and sales by providing tailored shopping experiences has a significant impact on the retail industry. By leveraging customer data to offer personalized product recommendations and customized promotions, retailers can create more meaningful and relevant interactions with their customers. This personalized approach enhances the shopping experience, making it more enjoyable and convenient for each individual. As a result, customers are more likely to return, leading to increased loyalty and repeat business. Additionally, tailored shopping experiences drive higher sales by presenting customers with products and offers that align with their preferences and needs, ultimately boosting overall revenue and profitability for retailers.

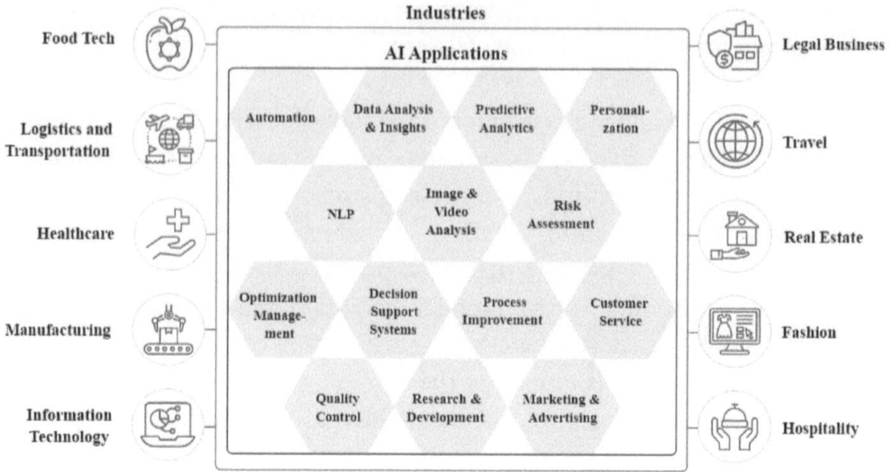

Real-World Applications in Different Industries

Conclusion

Data analytics and the Industrial Internet of Things (IIoT) are revolutionizing various industries by enhancing efficiency, reducing costs, and improving overall performance. By leveraging real-time data and advanced analytics, businesses can make informed decisions, optimize operations, and stay competitive in a rapidly evolving landscape. These technologies enable predictive maintenance, streamline supply chains, and improve product quality, driving innovation and productivity. As industries continue to adopt data-driven strategies and IIoT solutions, they can achieve greater operational efficiency, sustainability, and resilience in the face of changing market demands.

CHAPTER TWENTY

EMERGING TECHNOLOGIES

Emerging technologies are continuously reshaping our world, driving innovation and creating new opportunities across various industries. Some of the most impactful emerging technologies include artificial intelligence (AI), which enables advanced data analysis and automation; blockchain, which provides secure and transparent transaction records; the Internet of Things (IoT), connecting devices for enhanced communication and control; 5G technology, offering faster and more reliable connectivity; and biotechnology, revolutionizing healthcare and agriculture with breakthroughs in genetics and bioengineering. These technologies are transforming the way we live, work, and interact, paving the way for a more connected, efficient, and innovative future. Here are some of the most impactful emerging technologies:

1. **Artificial Intelligence (AI) and Machine Learning (ML)** are transformative technologies that enable computers to learn from data and make intelligent decisions. AI encompasses a broad range of applications, from natural language processing and image recognition to autonomous vehicles and robotics. Machine Learning, a subset of AI, focuses on developing algorithms that allow systems to learn and improve from experience. By analyzing vast amounts of data, AI and ML can identify patterns, predict outcomes, and optimize processes. These technologies drive innovation across various industries, enhancing efficiency, accuracy, and productivity while opening new opportunities for automation and advanced problem-solving.

- **Applications:** AI and ML are revolutionizing fields such as healthcare, finance, and transportation by enabling advanced data analysis, predictive modeling, and automation. In healthcare, they are used for diagnosing diseases, personalized treatment plans, and predicting patient outcomes. In finance, AI and ML enhance fraud detection, algorithmic trading, and risk management. In transportation, these technologies enable autonomous vehicles, optimize route planning, and improve traffic management. By leveraging vast amounts of data, AI and ML provide valuable insights, increase efficiency, and drive innovation across these sectors, ultimately transforming the way we live and work.
- **Impact:** These technologies are improving decision-making, enhancing customer experiences, and driving efficiency in various processes. AI and ML provide valuable insights by analyzing vast amounts of data, enabling more informed and accurate decisions. They personalize customer experiences through targeted recommendations and customized services, increasing satisfaction and loyalty. Additionally, automation and predictive modeling streamline operations, reduce costs, and enhance productivity across industries. Overall, the impact of AI and ML is profound, transforming businesses and improving outcomes in healthcare, finance, transportation, and beyond.

2. Quantum Computing leverages the principles of quantum mechanics to perform complex computations at unprecedented speeds. Unlike classical computers that use bits as units of information, quantum computers use qubits, which can represent multiple states simultaneously. This enables quantum computers to solve problems that are currently intractable for classical systems, such as cryptography, optimization, and complex simulations. By harnessing quantum entanglement and superposition, quantum computing has the potential to revolutionize fields such as materials science, drug discovery, and artificial intelligence, driving innovation and solving challenges that were previously beyond reach. Quantum computing is a revolutionary technology that harnesses the principles of quantum mechanics to perform computations at speeds unimaginable for classical computers. Unlike traditional systems that rely on binary bits (0s and 1s), quantum computers use quantum bits, or qubits, which can exist in multiple states simultaneously through the phenomenon known as superposition. This capability allows quantum computers to solve complex problems involving vast amounts of data, such as optimization tasks, cryptographic analysis, and molecular modeling, with extraordinary efficiency. Additionally, quantum entanglement and quantum interference further enhance their processing power, opening doors to transformative applications in fields like artificial intelligence, material science, and healthcare. While still in its developmental stages, quantum computing holds the promise of reshaping industries and driving scientific discovery

- **Applications:** Quantum computing has the potential to solve complex problems that are currently intractable for classical computers, such as cryptography, drug discovery, and optimization. By leveraging the principles of quantum mechanics, quantum computers can process information in ways that classical computers cannot, enabling them to perform calculations at unprecedented speeds. In cryptography, quantum computing can break traditional encryption methods, while also providing new ways to secure data. In drug discovery, it can simulate molecular interactions to identify potential treatments more efficiently. In optimization, quantum computing can tackle complex logistical problems, improving efficiency in various industries.
- **Impact:** Quantum computing promises to revolutionize industries by providing unprecedented computational power and speed. This advanced technology can tackle problems that are currently unsolvable by classical computers, enabling breakthroughs in areas such as cryptography, drug discovery, and optimization. By processing vast amounts of data more efficiently and accurately, quantum computing can drive innovation, enhance productivity, and open up new possibilities across various sectors. Its transformative impact has the potential to reshape industries, accelerate scientific research, and address complex challenges in ways that were previously unimaginable.

3. Blockchain is a decentralized digital ledger technology that enables secure and transparent recording of transactions. Each transaction is stored in a block, and these blocks are linked together in a chain, ensuring the integrity and immutability of the data. Blockchain has applications across various industries, including finance, supply chain, healthcare, and voting systems. It provides a reliable and tamper-proof method for tracking and verifying transactions, reducing the need for intermediaries and enhancing trust. By enabling secure and transparent data sharing, blockchain has the potential to revolutionize industries and drive innovation in areas such as digital identity, asset management, and smart contracts.

- **Applications:** Blockchain technology is transforming data management and security across industries, including finance, supply chain, and healthcare. In finance, it enables secure and transparent transactions, reducing fraud and improving efficiency. In the supply chain, blockchain provides real-time tracking and verification of goods, enhancing transparency and reducing delays. In healthcare, it ensures secure and tamper-proof storage of patient records, improving data integrity and accessibility. By providing a decentralized and immutable ledger, blockchain enhances trust, security, and efficiency across various sectors, driving innovation and improving overall operational effectiveness.
- **Impact:** Blockchain enables secure, transparent transactions without the need for intermediaries, significantly enhancing traceability and efficiency. By providing a decentralized and immutable ledger, blockchain ensures that transactions are recorded accurately and cannot be tampered with. This transparency builds trust among participants and reduces the risk of fraud. In industries like finance, supply chain, and healthcare, blockchain streamlines processes by eliminating the need for middlemen, resulting in faster and more cost-effective operations. Overall, the impact of blockchain technology is profound, driving innovation and improving the reliability and efficiency of various systems.

4. Edge Computing is a technology that processes data closer to the source of generation, rather than relying on centralized cloud-based systems. By performing computations at the network edge, where data is generated, edge computing reduces latency and bandwidth usage. This approach is particularly beneficial for applications requiring real-time processing, such as autonomous vehicles, IoT devices, and smart cities. By enabling faster data analysis and response times, edge computing enhances operational efficiency, improves user experiences, and supports the growing demand for low-latency applications in various industries.

- **Applications:** Edge computing brings computation closer to the data source, reducing latency and improving real-time processing for applications such as IoT devices and autonomous vehicles. By processing data at the network edge, where it is generated, edge computing minimizes the delay associated with sending data to centralized cloud-based systems. This results in faster response times and enhanced performance for applications that require real-time processing. Edge computing is particularly beneficial for scenarios where quick decision-making is crucial, such as in autonomous vehicles navigating traffic or IoT devices managing smart home systems.

- **Impact:**Edge computing enhances data privacy, reduces network congestion, and improves response times by processing data closer to its source. This decentralized approach minimizes the need to transmit sensitive information over long distances, thereby increasing data security. It also alleviates network congestion by reducing the volume of data sent to centralized servers. Furthermore, edge computing enables faster data analysis and response times, making it ideal for real-time applications such as autonomous vehicles and IoT devices. Overall, the impact of edge computing is significant, driving efficiency and reliability across various industries.

5. 5G Technology is the latest advancement in wireless communication, offering significantly faster speeds, lower latency, and greater capacity compared to previous generations. It enables seamless connectivity for a wide range of applications, from high-definition video streaming and immersive augmented reality experiences to smart cities and IoT devices. With its enhanced capabilities, 5G technology supports real-time data transmission, enabling innovations such as autonomous vehicles, remote healthcare, and smart infrastructure. By revolutionizing communication and connectivity, 5G technology is set to transform industries and improve the way we live and work.

- **Applications:** 5G technology provides faster and more reliable wireless communication, enabling significant advancements in various fields such as the Internet of Things (IoT), smart cities, and augmented reality (AR). With its high-speed data transmission and low latency, 5G supports the seamless connectivity required for IoT devices to communicate efficiently. In smart cities, 5G enables real-time monitoring and management of infrastructure, traffic, and public services, enhancing urban living. Additionally, augmented reality applications benefit from the increased bandwidth and reduced lag, offering more immersive and responsive experiences. Overall, 5G technology is revolutionizing connectivity and driving innovation across multiple industries.

- **Impact:** 5G technology supports the growth of connected devices and enhances the performance of data-intensive applications. By providing faster speeds, lower latency, and greater capacity, 5G enables seamless connectivity for a vast array of IoT devices, smart city infrastructure, and augmented reality experiences. This improved connectivity allows for real-time data transmission and analysis, facilitating the development of innovative applications and services. As a result, industries can leverage 5G to drive efficiency, productivity, and new opportunities, ultimately transforming the way we interact with technology and the world around us.

6. Augmented Reality (AR) and Virtual Reality (VR) are immersive technologies that enhance and simulate real-world environments. AR overlays digital information onto the physical world, enhancing the user's perception and interaction with their surroundings. VR creates entirely virtual environments, providing an immersive experience that can transport users to different places and scenarios. These technologies have applications in various fields, including gaming, education, training, and healthcare. AR and VR enable interactive and engaging experiences, improving learning outcomes, enhancing entertainment, and providing innovative solutions for training and therapy. Their impact is transformative, offering new ways to experience and interact with digital content.

- **Applications:** AR and VR are transforming industries such as gaming, education, and healthcare by providing immersive and interactive experiences. In gaming, they create realistic and engaging environments, enhancing gameplay and user interaction. In education, AR and VR offer virtual field trips, interactive simulations, and hands-on learning experiences that make lessons more engaging and effective. In healthcare, these technologies enable advanced training for medical professionals, virtual therapy sessions, and realistic surgical simulations. By immersing users in interactive digital worlds, AR and VR are revolutionizing how we learn, play, and receive care.

- **Impact:** These technologies enhance training, improve remote collaboration, and create new opportunities for entertainment and education. By offering immersive and interactive experiences, AR and VR provide realistic simulations and hands-on learning opportunities, improving the effectiveness of training programs. They facilitate remote collaboration by allowing individuals to interact in virtual environments, making meetings and teamwork more engaging and efficient. In entertainment and education, AR and VR create captivating and interactive content, offering new ways to learn and enjoy media. Overall, these technologies drive innovation and improve experiences across various fields.

7. Biotechnology leverages biological systems and organisms to develop innovative solutions and products across various sectors. It encompasses a wide range of applications, from genetic engineering and biopharmaceuticals to agriculture and environmental conservation. In healthcare, biotechnology enables the development of advanced therapies, personalized medicine, and diagnostic tools. In agriculture, it enhances crop yields, pest resistance, and sustainability. Biotechnology also plays a critical role in environmental conservation by developing biofuels and bioremediation techniques. By harnessing the power of biology, biotechnology drives innovation, improves quality of life, and addresses global challenges in health, agriculture, and the environment.

- **Applications:** Biotechnology is advancing fields such as genetic engineering, personalized medicine, and agricultural innovation. In genetic engineering, it allows for the modification of organisms' DNA to develop new traits and improve crop yields. Personalized medicine leverages biotechnological advancements to tailor treatments to individual patients based on their genetic profiles, enhancing efficacy and reducing side effects. Agricultural innovation benefits from biotechnology through the development of pest-resistant crops, improved livestock breeds, and sustainable farming practices. These applications drive progress in healthcare, agriculture, and other sectors, ultimately improving quality of life and addressing global challenges.
- **Impact:** Biotechnology improves healthcare outcomes, enhances food production, and addresses environmental challenges. By enabling the development of advanced therapies and personalized medicine, it

significantly impacts patient care and treatment effectiveness. In agriculture, biotechnology boosts crop yields, improves pest resistance, and promotes sustainable farming practices, ensuring a more reliable and efficient food supply. Additionally, biotechnological solutions like biofuels and bioremediation help mitigate environmental issues, contributing to cleaner and more sustainable ecosystems. Overall, the impact of biotechnology is profound, driving progress and innovation in multiple sectors.

8. Autonomous Vehicles Autonomous vehicles, also known as self-driving cars, are revolutionizing transportation by leveraging advanced sensors, artificial intelligence, and machine learning algorithms to navigate and operate without human intervention. These vehicles have the potential to enhance road safety, reduce traffic congestion, and improve fuel efficiency. By continuously analyzing real-time data from their surroundings, autonomous vehicles can make precise and informed decisions, leading to a more efficient and reliable transportation system. The widespread adoption of autonomous vehicles promises to transform the way we travel, making transportation safer, more convenient, and environmentally friendly.

- **Applications:** Autonomous vehicles are being developed for personal transportation, logistics, and public transit. In personal transportation, self-driving cars offer convenience and safety by reducing the risk of human error. In logistics, autonomous trucks and delivery drones can optimize supply chain operations, ensuring timely and efficient delivery of goods. In public transit, autonomous buses and shuttles can improve the reliability and accessibility of transportation services, reducing congestion and enhancing urban mobility. By leveraging advanced technologies, autonomous vehicles have the potential to transform the transportation landscape and create more efficient, safe, and sustainable systems.
- **Impact:** Autonomous vehicles promise to improve road safety, reduce traffic congestion, and enhance mobility for individuals with disabilities. By leveraging advanced sensors and AI, these vehicles can reduce the risk of human error, leading to fewer accidents. Their efficient route planning and real-time traffic management capabilities can alleviate congestion, making transportation more fluid. Additionally, autonomous

vehicles offer increased independence and accessibility for individuals with disabilities, providing them with safer and more reliable transportation options. Overall, the impact of autonomous vehicles is transformative, enhancing the safety, efficiency, and inclusivity of our transportation systems.

9. Renewable Energy Technologies harness natural resources such as sunlight, wind, and water to generate sustainable and clean energy. These technologies, including solar panels, wind turbines, and hydropower systems, offer environmentally friendly alternatives to fossil fuels, reducing greenhouse gas emissions and mitigating climate change. Renewable energy sources are abundant and can be replenished naturally, ensuring long-term energy security. By transitioning to renewable energy, we can decrease our reliance on finite resources, promote energy independence, and create a more sustainable and resilient energy infrastructure for the future.

- **Applications:** Innovations in solar, wind, and energy storage technologies are driving the transition to sustainable energy sources. Solar panels and wind turbines capture renewable energy from the sun and wind, providing clean and abundant power. Advanced energy storage solutions, such as batteries and pumped hydro storage, ensure a stable supply of energy by storing excess power for use during periods of low generation. These advancements in renewable energy technologies enable a shift away from fossil fuels, reduce greenhouse gas emissions, and promote a more sustainable and environmentally friendly energy infrastructure.
- **Impact:** Renewable energy technologies reduce reliance on fossil fuels, decrease greenhouse gas emissions, and promote environmental sustainability. By harnessing clean and abundant natural resources such as sunlight and wind, these technologies provide a sustainable alternative to finite fossil fuels. This shift helps mitigate climate change, improve air quality, and preserve ecosystems. Additionally, renewable energy promotes energy independence and resilience, ensuring a reliable and sustainable energy supply for future generations. Overall, the impact of renewable energy technologies is transformative, driving positive environmental and economic outcomes.

10. Advanced Robotics leverages cutting-edge technologies such as artificial intelligence, machine learning, and sensors to create intelligent and autonomous machines capable of performing complex tasks. These robots are used in a variety of applications, from manufacturing and logistics to healthcare and exploration. In manufacturing, robots improve efficiency and precision on assembly lines. In logistics, they streamline warehouse operations and delivery processes. In healthcare, robots assist in surgeries, rehabilitation, and patient care. By enhancing capabilities and automating tasks, advanced robotics is transforming industries, improving productivity, and opening new possibilities for innovation and human-robot collaboration.

- **Applications:** Advanced robotics are being used in manufacturing, healthcare, and service industries to perform tasks with precision and efficiency. In manufacturing, robots enhance productivity and accuracy on assembly lines. In healthcare, they assist in surgeries, rehabilitation, and patient care, improving outcomes and reducing human error. In the service industries, advanced robotics streamline processes such as delivery, cleaning, and customer service, providing consistent and reliable performance. By automating complex tasks and enhancing operational efficiency, advanced robotics is transforming various sectors and driving innovation.
- **Impact:** Advanced robotics enhance productivity, improve safety, and enable new capabilities across various sectors. By automating complex and repetitive tasks, robots increase efficiency and precision, leading to higher productivity. They also improve workplace safety by taking over dangerous and physically demanding jobs, reducing the risk of injuries. Additionally, advanced robotics enable new capabilities, such as remote surgery, autonomous logistics, and personalized customer service, transforming industries and driving innovation. Overall, the impact of advanced robotics is significant, revolutionizing how we work, live, and interact with technology.

CHAPTER TWENTY-ONE

SUSTAINABILITY AND GREEN MANUFACTURING

Sustainability and green manufacturing focus on creating products and processes that minimize environmental impact, conserve resources, and ensure long-term ecological balance. This involves using eco-friendly materials, reducing waste, and implementing energy-efficient technologies. Sustainable manufacturing practices include recycling, reusing materials, and designing products with a longer lifespan. The benefits of these practices include reduced carbon emissions, lower operational costs, and improved public health. By adopting sustainable and green manufacturing, industries can contribute to environmental preservation, promote resource conservation, and create a more sustainable future for generations to come.

Sustainability and green manufacturing represent the commitment to producing goods while prioritizing environmental responsibility and resource conservation. By integrating eco-friendly practices such as energy efficiency, waste reduction, and the use of renewable materials, green manufacturing seeks to minimize the environmental footprint of industrial activities. Sustainability goes further, emphasizing long-term strategies like creating circular economies, promoting social responsibility, and ensuring that current advancements do not compromise future generations' ability to thrive. Together, these approaches not only preserve natural resources and mitigate climate change but also drive innovation, reduce costs, and enhance market competitiveness, demonstrating the critical role of industrial engineering in shaping a greener, more sustainable world.

Principles of Green Manufacturing: The principles of green manufacturing involve creating products and processes that reduce environmental impact, conserve resources, and promote sustainability. These principles include using eco-friendly materials, minimizing waste, optimizing energy efficiency, and implementing recycling and reuse strategies. Green manufacturing also emphasizes designing products with a longer lifespan and ensuring that production processes are safe for both workers and the environment. By adopting these principles, industries can achieve greater resource efficiency, reduce carbon emissions, and contribute to a more sustainable and environmentally friendly economy.

Green Manufacturing is guided by several core principles that aim to balance economic production with environmental responsibility. It emphasizes energy efficiency, striving to reduce consumption by utilizing renewable energy sources and optimizing operational processes. Another key principle is waste minimization, which involves reducing, reusing, and recycling materials to lower the environmental footprint of industrial activities. Green manufacturing also prioritizes eco-design, ensuring products are created with sustainability in mind throughout their lifecycle—from raw materials to disposal. Pollution prevention is fundamental, advocating for cleaner production methods and technologies that limit emissions and environmental impact. Lastly, the principle of sustainability underpins green manufacturing, focusing on long-term solutions such as circular economies, which promote continuous reuse of resources, ensuring future generations can thrive. Together, these principles form the blueprint for a cleaner, greener industrial future.

1. Resource Efficiency: Resource efficiency in green manufacturing focuses on maximizing the use of materials and energy to minimize waste and reduce environmental impact. This involves optimizing production processes, utilizing renewable resources, and implementing recycling and reuse strategies. By improving resource efficiency, manufacturers can lower operational costs, decrease carbon emissions, and conserve natural resources. Additionally, it promotes sustainable practices that contribute to long-term ecological balance and environmental preservation. Overall, resource efficiency is a key principle in achieving sustainable and green manufacturing goals.

Resource efficiency focuses on optimizing the use of natural and human resources to achieve maximum productivity while minimizing waste and environmental impact. This principle involves reducing the consumption of raw materials, energy, and water during manufacturing and operational processes, ensuring that resources are used wisely and sustainably. It also emphasizes adopting innovative technologies, such as energy-efficient machinery and digital tools, to streamline workflows and reduce unnecessary resource expenditure. By prioritizing resource efficiency, industries can not only lower their production costs but also contribute to environmental conservation, creating a balance between economic growth and ecological responsibility. This approach forms a cornerstone of sustainable and green manufacturing practices.

- **Material Conservation:** Material conservation focuses on using materials more efficiently by reducing waste, reusing scraps, and recycling. By optimizing material usage, manufacturers can minimize their environmental impact, lower costs, and conserve natural resources. Implementing practices such as reusing production scraps and incorporating recycled materials into new products helps reduce the amount of waste sent to landfills. Additionally, material conservation supports sustainable production processes and promotes a circular economy, where resources are continually reused and repurposed, contributing to long-term ecological balance and sustainability. Material conservation emphasizes the responsible and efficient use of materials to minimize waste and preserve natural resources. It involves adopting practices such as reusing and recycling materials, substituting scarce resources with sustainable alternatives, and designing products to maximize material efficiency throughout their lifecycle. By prioritizing material conservation, industries can reduce costs, decrease environmental impact, and contribute to a circular economy, where resources are continually repurposed rather than discarded. This approach not only supports sustainability but also ensures long-term resource availability, making it a critical principle for modern manufacturing and industrial engineering.
- **Energy Efficiency:** Energy efficiency focuses on implementing energy-saving technologies and practices to reduce energy consumption. This involves optimizing production processes, upgrading equipment to more energy-efficient models, and utilizing renewable energy sources. By reducing energy consumption, manufacturers can lower operational costs, decrease greenhouse gas emissions, and contribute to environmental sustainability. Energy efficiency also promotes the

responsible use of resources and supports efforts to combat climate change. Overall, prioritizing energy efficiency is a key aspect of sustainable and green manufacturing, leading to long-term ecological benefits and economic savings. Energy efficiency is the practice of optimizing energy use to achieve maximum productivity while reducing waste and environmental impact. It involves utilizing advanced technologies, such as energy-efficient machinery, automation, and smart systems, to minimize energy consumption during manufacturing and operational processes. By implementing energy management strategies and investing in renewable energy sources, industries can lower costs, decrease greenhouse gas emissions, and enhance sustainability. Energy efficiency is a cornerstone of green manufacturing, enabling businesses to balance environmental responsibility with economic growth and contribute to a cleaner, more sustainable future.

2. Pollution Prevention: Pollution prevention focuses on reducing or eliminating the release of harmful pollutants into the environment. This involves implementing practices and technologies that minimize waste generation, control emissions, and prevent the contamination of air, water, and soil. By adopting cleaner production processes, using eco-friendly materials, and improving waste management, manufacturers can significantly reduce their environmental footprint. Pollution prevention not only protects natural ecosystems and public health but also promotes sustainable development by conserving resources and ensuring a cleaner, safer environment for future generations. Pollution prevention focuses on reducing or eliminating waste and harmful emissions at their source rather than managing them after they are created. This proactive approach involves adopting cleaner production techniques, using eco-friendly materials, and implementing advanced technologies to minimize environmental impact. Strategies such as optimizing manufacturing processes, reducing resource consumption, and substituting hazardous substances with safer alternatives play a crucial role in this effort. Pollution prevention not only benefits the environment by conserving natural ecosystems and reducing air, water, and soil contamination but also provides economic advantages through cost savings and improved efficiency. As a cornerstone of sustainable practices, it emphasizes the importance of protecting the planet while maintaining industrial growth and innovation.

- **Emission Reduction:** Emission reduction focuses on reducing air, water, and soil pollution through cleaner production techniques. This involves implementing advanced technologies and practices that minimize the release of harmful pollutants and waste into the environment. By optimizing industrial processes, using eco-friendly materials, and enhancing waste management systems, manufacturers can significantly decrease emissions and prevent contamination. Emission reduction not only protects natural ecosystems and public health but also supports sustainable development by conserving resources and promoting a cleaner, healthier environment for future generations. Emission reduction involves implementing strategies to minimize the release of harmful pollutants, such as greenhouse gases and industrial byproducts, into the environment. This can be achieved through the adoption of cleaner production technologies, energy-efficient equipment, and renewable energy sources to reduce reliance on fossil fuels. Additionally, emission reduction emphasizes process optimization to lower waste output and the use of carbon capture and storage technologies to prevent harmful emissions from entering the atmosphere. By reducing emissions, industries not only mitigate climate change and protect ecosystems but also comply with environmental regulations and enhance their reputation for sustainability. This proactive approach is essential for fostering a healthier planet and promoting long-term industrial growth.
- **Waste Management:** focuses on implementing proper practices to minimize and safely dispose of industrial waste. This involves reducing waste generation at the source, promoting recycling and reuse of materials, and ensuring the safe handling and disposal of hazardous substances. By adopting efficient waste management strategies, manufacturers can minimize their environmental impact, conserve resources, and reduce costs associated with waste disposal. Effective waste management also helps prevent pollution, protect public health, and promote a cleaner and more sustainable environment. Waste management focuses on the efficient handling, reduction, and disposal of waste to minimize its environmental impact. It involves a systematic approach that includes waste segregation, recycling, reuse, and safe disposal to ensure sustainability. Key strategies include reducing waste generation at the source, optimizing processes to minimize excess, and implementing circular economy practices where materials are

continuously repurposed rather than discarded. Proper waste management not only conserves natural resources and reduces pollution but also enhances operational efficiency and complies with environmental regulations. It plays a crucial role in fostering a cleaner and more sustainable future while supporting industrial growth and innovation.

3. Lifecycle Perspective: A lifecycle perspective in green manufacturing considers the environmental impact of a product from its inception to its disposal. This holistic approach involves evaluating each stage of the product's life, including raw material extraction, production, distribution, use, and end-of-life management. By assessing the entire lifecycle, manufacturers can identify opportunities to reduce resource consumption, minimize waste, and enhance sustainability. Implementing lifecycle thinking helps ensure that products are designed and produced with minimal environmental impact, promoting long-term ecological balance and reducing the overall carbon footprint. A lifecycle perspective emphasizes evaluating the environmental, economic, and social impacts of a product or process throughout its entire lifecycle—from raw material extraction and manufacturing to usage, disposal, and recycling. This approach ensures that sustainability is integrated into every stage, identifying opportunities to reduce resource consumption, waste, and emissions while maximizing efficiency and value. By considering the lifecycle, industries can make informed decisions that minimize negative impacts on the environment, enhance the durability and recyclability of products, and support a circular economy. Adopting a lifecycle perspective helps align industrial practices with sustainable development goals, fostering a balanced and responsible approach to production and consumption.

- **Product Design:** Product design involves creating products with their entire lifecycle in mind, including material selection, production, use, and end-of-life disposal. This approach ensures that environmental impact is minimized at every stage. By choosing sustainable materials, optimizing production processes, and designing for durability and recyclability, manufacturers can reduce waste and conserve resources. Considering the entire lifecycle helps create eco-friendly products that are easier to recycle or repurpose at the end of their use, promoting sustainability and reducing the overall carbon footprint. This comprehensive strategy contributes to long-term ecological balance and environmental responsibility. Product design is the process of creating and developing products that meet functional, aesthetic, and sustainability criteria while addressing consumer needs and expectations. It involves considering factors such as materials, manufacturing methods, usability, and environmental impact throughout the product's lifecycle. In green manufacturing, product design emphasizes eco-friendly practices, such as using renewable or recyclable materials, reducing energy consumption during production, and ensuring the product's end-of-life disposal aligns with sustainability goals. By integrating innovation, efficiency, and environmental responsibility, product design not only enhances the product's appeal but also contributes to building a greener and more sustainable future.

- **Circular Economy:** A circular economy encourages the continual reuse and recycling of products and materials to minimize waste and conserve resources. This approach focuses on designing products for longevity, reparability, and recyclability, ensuring that materials can be reused in new products at the end of their life cycle. By creating closed-loop systems, the circular economy reduces the need for virgin resources, decreases environmental impact, and promotes sustainable production and consumption patterns. This holistic strategy supports long-term ecological balance, resource conservation, and a more sustainable future. The circular economy is an innovative approach to production and consumption that seeks to minimize waste and maximize the reuse of resources. Unlike the traditional linear model of "take, make, dispose," the circular economy focuses on creating closed-loop systems where materials, components, and products are continuously repurposed. This involves designing products with durability, repairability, and recyclability in mind, as well as implementing processes to recover and reuse waste from production or post-consumer use. By prioritizing resource efficiency, reducing environmental impact, and fostering sustainable practices, the circular economy supports long-term economic growth while preserving natural ecosystems, ensuring a balanced approach to industrial development and ecological responsibility.

Practices in Green Manufacturing: Practices in green manufacturing involve adopting sustainable methods that minimize environmental impact and promote resource conservation. Key practices include using eco-friendly materials, optimizing energy efficiency, and reducing waste through recycling and reuse. Manufacturers implement cleaner production techniques to reduce emissions and pollution, while also focusing on efficient waste management to safely handle and dispose of industrial waste. Additionally, adopting a lifecycle perspective ensures that products are designed with sustainability in mind, from material selection to end-of-life disposal. By embracing these practices, green manufacturing supports environmental preservation and promotes long-term ecological balance. Green manufacturing practices focus on reducing the environmental impact of production processes while maintaining economic and operational efficiency. These practices include the adoption of energy-efficient technologies, the use of renewable energy sources, and the implementation of waste reduction strategies such as recycling and reusing materials. Eco-friendly product design is a key element, ensuring that products are manufactured using sustainable materials and designed for durability, repairability, and end-of-life recyclability. Pollution prevention techniques, such as cleaner production methods and emissions control, are also integral to green manufacturing. Additionally, businesses often engage in sustainable supply chain management, working with partners who uphold environmental responsibility. By integrating these practices, green manufacturing promotes sustainability, conserves natural resources, and supports long-term industrial growth.

1. Eco-Design: Eco-design focuses on creating products with minimal environmental impact throughout their lifecycle. This involves selecting sustainable materials, reducing energy consumption during production, and designing for durability and recyclability. By considering the entire lifecycle—from raw material extraction to disposal—eco-design aims to minimize waste, conserve resources, and reduce pollution. Implementing eco-design principles helps manufacturers create environmentally friendly products that promote sustainability and support a circular economy, ultimately contributing to a healthier planet and long-term ecological balance. Eco-design is an innovative approach to product development that prioritizes environmental sustainability throughout a product's lifecycle. It involves designing products to minimize their ecological impact by using renewable or recyclable materials, reducing energy consumption during production, and ensuring the product's durability and reparability. Eco-design also considers the end-of-life phase, promoting ease of recycling or safe disposal. By integrating sustainability into every stage of product creation, eco-design not only reduces waste and conserves natural resources but also enhances market competitiveness by meeting the growing demand for environmentally friendly products. This practice plays a vital role in advancing green manufacturing and fostering a more sustainable future.

- **Sustainable Materials:** Sustainable materials focus on using renewable, biodegradable, or recycled materials in product design. By incorporating these eco-friendly materials, manufacturers can reduce their reliance on finite resources, minimize environmental impact, and promote resource conservation. Renewable materials, such as bamboo or organic cotton, are naturally replenished, while biodegradable materials break down naturally, reducing waste. Recycled materials, like reclaimed plastics or metals, help divert waste from landfills and reduce the need for new raw materials. Using sustainable materials supports a circular economy and contributes to long-term ecological balance and environmental sustainability. Sustainable materials are those that are sourced, produced, and used in ways that minimize negative environmental impacts while conserving natural resources for future generations. These materials often include renewable resources, such as bamboo or hemp, that regenerate quickly, as well as recycled materials like reclaimed wood or recycled plastics, which reduce waste and pollution. Sustainable materials are chosen for their durability, low energy requirements during production, and potential for recycling or biodegrading at the end of their lifecycle. By integrating these materials into manufacturing and construction, industries can reduce their carbon footprint, promote eco-friendly practices, and contribute to a circular economy, paving the way for a more sustainable future.
- **Design for Disassembly:** Design for disassembly involves creating products that can be easily taken apart for recycling or reuse at the end of their lifecycle. This approach focuses on using modular components, standardized fasteners, and materials that can be separated without damage. By designing products for disassembly, manufacturers can facilitate efficient recycling, reduce waste, and promote a circular economy. This strategy helps conserve resources, minimize

environmental impact, and ensure that products contribute to sustainability throughout their entire lifecycle. Design for Disassembly (DfD) is a sustainable design approach that focuses on creating products that can be easily taken apart at the end of their life cycle. This method enables components and materials to be reused, recycled, or safely disposed of, reducing waste and conserving resources. DfD incorporates modular design principles, standardized connections, and clear labeling to simplify the disassembly process. By prioritizing materials that are non-toxic and recyclable, and minimizing the use of adhesives or permanent fasteners, DfD aligns with circular economy principles. This approach not only supports environmental sustainability but also offers economic benefits by recovering valuable materials, making it a crucial element of green manufacturing practices.

2. Energy Management: Energy management focuses on implementing strategies and technologies to optimize energy use and reduce consumption. This involves monitoring and controlling energy usage, upgrading to energy-efficient equipment, and utilizing renewable energy sources. By improving energy management, manufacturers can lower operational costs, decrease greenhouse gas emissions, and enhance overall sustainability. Effective energy management promotes responsible resource use, supports efforts to combat climate change, and contributes to a more sustainable and efficient manufacturing process. Energy management is a strategic approach to optimizing energy usage in industrial and operational processes to maximize efficiency while minimizing costs and environmental impact. It involves monitoring and analyzing energy consumption patterns to identify areas for improvement, implementing energy-efficient technologies, and integrating renewable energy sources. Effective energy management includes setting energy reduction targets, adopting smart systems to regulate energy use, and ensuring compliance with environmental standards. By reducing unnecessary energy waste and enhancing efficiency, energy management not only supports sustainable practices but also contributes to long-term economic savings and a greener, more resilient industrial future.

- **Renewable Energy Sources:** Utilizing renewable energy sources, such as solar, wind, and hydropower, to power manufacturing operations is a key practice in green manufacturing. By harnessing these clean and sustainable energy sources, manufacturers can reduce their reliance on fossil fuels, lower greenhouse gas emissions, and decrease their overall environmental footprint. Implementing renewable energy technologies not only promotes environmental sustainability but also provides long-term cost savings and energy security. This transition to renewable energy supports the development of a more sustainable and resilient manufacturing sector, contributing to a healthier planet and a sustainable future. Renewable energy sources are natural, inexhaustible resources that generate energy without depleting the planet's reserves or harming the environment. These include solar energy, harnessed from sunlight; wind energy, captured through turbines; hydroelectric power, generated from flowing water; and geothermal energy, extracted from the Earth's internal heat. Biomass, derived from organic materials, is another renewable source contributing to sustainable energy production. These energy sources offer an alternative to fossil fuels by reducing greenhouse gas emissions and mitigating climate change impacts. Their integration into industries and households supports sustainability, drives technological innovation, and promotes energy independence for a cleaner and more resilient future.

- **Energy-Efficient Equipment:** Investing in energy-efficient machinery and optimizing production processes to reduce energy consumption are essential practices in green manufacturing. By upgrading to modern, energy-efficient equipment, manufacturers can significantly lower their energy usage, reduce operational costs, and decrease greenhouse gas emissions. Additionally, optimizing production processes through automation, process improvements, and regular maintenance ensures that equipment operates at peak efficiency. These measures contribute to a more sustainable and environmentally friendly manufacturing sector, promoting resource conservation and supporting efforts to combat climate change. Energy-efficient equipment refers to machinery and devices designed to perform tasks using minimal energy while maintaining high levels of productivity. These tools incorporate advanced technologies such as improved insulation, smart sensors, and optimized motors to reduce power consumption during operation. By replacing conventional equipment with energy-efficient alternatives, industries can significantly lower their energy costs, decrease greenhouse gas emissions, and contribute to sustainability efforts. Additionally, the use of energy-efficient equipment supports regulatory compliance with environmental standards and enhances operational efficiency, making it a cornerstone of green manufacturing and sustainable industrial practices.

3. Waste Reduction: Waste reduction focuses on minimizing waste generation and promoting efficient use of materials. This involves implementing practices such as recycling, reusing materials, and reducing excess production. By adopting waste reduction strategies, manufacturers can lower their environmental impact, conserve resources, and reduce disposal costs. Effective waste reduction also supports a circular economy, where materials are continually reused and repurposed, minimizing the need for new raw materials. Overall, waste reduction contributes to a more sustainable manufacturing process and helps protect the environment. Waste reduction is a fundamental aspect of sustainable manufacturing that aims to minimize the generation of waste at every stage of the production process. This involves optimizing resource utilization, improving operational efficiency, and adopting practices such as lean manufacturing and just-in-time inventory management to eliminate excess materials and redundancies. Recycling and reusing byproducts or scrap materials further contribute to reducing landfill waste. Additionally, innovative product designs and smarter packaging solutions can significantly cut down on unnecessary material use. Waste reduction not only conserves natural resources and reduces environmental impact but also lowers operational costs, making it a vital component of green and sustainable industrial practices.

- **Lean Manufacturing:** Lean manufacturing involves implementing principles and practices that minimize waste and improve efficiency in production processes. This approach focuses on identifying and eliminating non-value-added activities, streamlining operations, and optimizing resource utilization. By reducing excess inventory, shortening production cycles, and improving workflow, lean manufacturing enhances productivity and lowers costs. Additionally, it promotes continuous improvement and fosters a culture of sustainability by minimizing environmental impact and conserving resources. Adopting lean manufacturing principles helps manufacturers achieve higher efficiency, better quality, and increased competitiveness in the market.

- **Closed-Loop Systems:** Closed-loop systems focus on creating processes where waste products are reused within the production cycle, minimizing waste and conserving resources. In these systems, materials and by-products generated during manufacturing are captured, processed, and reintegrated into the production process. This approach reduces the need for new raw materials, decreases environmental impact, and promotes resource efficiency. By implementing closed-loop systems, manufacturers can achieve greater sustainability, lower production costs, and contribute to a circular economy where resources are continuously reused and repurposed, supporting long-term ecological balance.

4. Water Conservation: Water conservation involves implementing strategies to reduce water usage and promote efficient water management in manufacturing processes. This includes using water-saving technologies, recycling and reusing water, and optimizing production processes to minimize water consumption. By conserving water, manufacturers can lower operational costs, reduce their environmental impact, and contribute to the sustainable management of water resources. Effective water conservation practices support environmental sustainability, ensure a reliable water supply, and promote long-term ecological balance.

- **Water Recycling:** Water recycling involves implementing systems to treat and reuse water within manufacturing processes, significantly reducing freshwater consumption. By capturing and treating wastewater, manufacturers can recycle it for various uses, such as cooling, cleaning, or production processes. This approach conserves water resources, lowers operational costs, and minimizes environmental impact. Effective water recycling systems support sustainable water management, promote resource efficiency, and contribute to long-term ecological balance by reducing the demand for freshwater and decreasing wastewater discharge.
- **Efficient Water Use:** Efficient water use involves employing processes and technologies that minimize water waste in manufacturing operations. This includes optimizing production techniques, implementing water-saving devices, and adopting practices that reduce water consumption. By using water efficiently, manufacturers can lower operational costs, conserve vital water resources, and minimize their

environmental impact. This approach supports sustainable water management, ensuring a reliable water supply and promoting long-term ecological balance. Efficient water use is crucial in creating a more sustainable and environmentally friendly manufacturing sector.

Benefits of Green Manufacturing: Green manufacturing offers numerous benefits, including reduced environmental impact, cost savings, and improved public health. By minimizing waste, conserving resources, and reducing emissions, green manufacturing helps protect natural ecosystems and combat climate change. Additionally, adopting sustainable practices can lead to lower operational costs through increased efficiency and reduced material and energy consumption. Green manufacturing also promotes a positive brand image, attracting environmentally conscious consumers and enhancing market competitiveness. Overall, the benefits of green manufacturing contribute to a healthier planet, economic savings, and a sustainable future for generations to come.

1. Environmental Benefits: Green manufacturing offers significant environmental benefits by reducing pollution, conserving natural resources, and minimizing waste. By adopting eco-friendly practices, such as using sustainable materials, optimizing energy efficiency, and implementing recycling and reuse strategies, manufacturers can decrease their environmental footprint. These efforts contribute to the protection of natural ecosystems, reduction of greenhouse gas emissions, and preservation of biodiversity. Additionally, green manufacturing helps combat climate change by promoting sustainable production and consumption patterns, ultimately leading to a healthier and more balanced environment for future generations.

- **Reduced Carbon Footprint:** Reduced carbon footprint involves lowering greenhouse gas emissions to mitigate climate change. By adopting energy-efficient technologies, utilizing renewable energy sources, and implementing sustainable practices, manufacturers can significantly decrease their carbon emissions. These efforts help reduce the impact of industrial activities on global warming and contribute to a healthier, more sustainable environment. Lowering the carbon footprint not only supports climate change mitigation but also enhances a company's reputation and compliance with environmental regulations, promoting long-term ecological balance and sustainability.

- **Resource Conservation:** Resource conservation focuses on preserving natural resources to ensure their availability for future generations. This involves implementing sustainable practices, such as reducing waste, recycling, and using renewable materials, to minimize the depletion of finite resources. By conserving resources, manufacturers can protect ecosystems, reduce environmental impact, and promote long-term ecological balance. Resource conservation supports the responsible use of natural resources, ensuring that they remain available for future generations to meet their needs and sustain a healthy environment.

2. Economic Benefits: Green manufacturing offers numerous economic benefits, including cost savings, increased efficiency, and enhanced competitiveness. By reducing waste, conserving resources, and optimizing energy use, manufacturers can lower operational costs and improve profitability. Additionally, sustainable practices can attract environmentally conscious consumers, leading to increased market share and customer loyalty. Green manufacturing also supports compliance with environmental regulations, reducing the risk of fines and penalties. Overall, the economic benefits of green manufacturing contribute to a more sustainable and resilient business model, promoting long-term growth and success.

- **Cost Savings:** Cost savings in green manufacturing are achieved by reducing energy consumption, minimizing waste, and conserving resources. By implementing energy-efficient technologies, optimizing production processes, and recycling materials, manufacturers can lower operational costs and increase efficiency. These practices not only reduce expenses but also improve profitability and sustainability. Efficient use of resources and waste reduction contribute to significant cost savings, making green manufacturing an economically viable and environmentally responsible approach.
- **Market Competitiveness:** Market competitiveness is enhanced by meeting the growing demand for sustainable products. As consumers increasingly seek environmentally friendly options, manufacturers that adopt green practices and produce sustainable products can gain a significant competitive edge. This approach not only attracts eco-conscious customers but also builds brand loyalty and reputation. By staying ahead of market trends and regulatory requirements, companies can differentiate themselves from competitors, secure a larger market

share, and achieve long-term success in a rapidly evolving market landscape. Embracing sustainability fosters innovation, reduces risks, and aligns with the values of today's discerning consumers.

3. Social Benefits: Green manufacturing provides significant social benefits by improving public health, enhancing community well-being, and creating job opportunities. By reducing pollution and minimizing the release of harmful substances, green manufacturing helps protect the health of workers and local communities. Additionally, sustainable practices promote a healthier environment, contributing to the overall well-being of society. Green manufacturing also fosters economic development by creating green jobs and supporting local economies. These social benefits contribute to a more equitable, healthy, and sustainable future for all.

- **Health and Safety:** Improving workplace health and safety involves reducing exposure to harmful substances through the adoption of green manufacturing practices. By minimizing the use of toxic chemicals and implementing cleaner production methods, manufacturers can create a safer working environment for employees. This not only protects workers from health risks and occupational hazards but also enhances overall well-being and productivity. Prioritizing health and safety in manufacturing supports a healthier workforce, reduces medical costs, and fosters a culture of safety and environmental responsibility.
- **Community Impact:** Community impact involves contributing to the well-being of communities by reducing pollution and conserving resources through green manufacturing practices. By adopting sustainable methods, manufacturers can minimize emissions and waste, resulting in cleaner air and water for local populations. Additionally, conserving resources ensures the availability of vital materials for future generations, promoting long-term environmental health. These efforts foster healthier, more resilient communities, enhance the quality of life, and demonstrate corporate social responsibility. Ultimately, green manufacturing supports the overall well-being of society and promotes a sustainable future for all.

Case Studies: Case studies in green manufacturing demonstrate the successful implementation of sustainable practices by various companies. These examples highlight the tangible benefits of adopting eco-friendly methods, such as cost savings, reduced environmental impact, and enhanced market competitiveness. By showcasing real-world applications, case studies provide valuable insights into the strategies and technologies that drive sustainable manufacturing. They also serve as a source of inspiration and guidance for other businesses seeking to transition to greener practices. Overall, case studies illustrate the positive outcomes of green manufacturing and encourage wider adoption of sustainable methods in the industry.

1. Tesla: Tesla's Gigafactories exemplify sustainable practices by being highly efficient and utilizing renewable energy sources such as solar and wind power. The company prioritizes a circular economy approach, focusing on recycling batteries and incorporating sustainable materials in its vehicles. By adopting these eco-friendly practices, Tesla reduces its environmental impact, lowers greenhouse gas emissions, and contributes to a more sustainable and responsible manufacturing process, aligning with its mission to accelerate the world's transition to sustainable energy.

- **Sustainable Practices:** Tesla's Gigafactories exemplify sustainable practices by being highly efficient and utilizing renewable energy sources like solar and wind power. These facilities are designed to minimize environmental impact and energy consumption through advanced manufacturing techniques. By integrating renewable energy and optimizing efficiency, Tesla significantly reduces greenhouse gas emissions and supports its mission to accelerate the transition to sustainable energy.
- **Circular Economy:** Tesla prioritizes a circular economy by recycling batteries and incorporating sustainable materials in its vehicles. This approach ensures that valuable resources are reused, reducing the need for new raw materials and minimizing environmental impact. By focusing on recycling and sustainability, Tesla promotes resource conservation, lowers waste generation, and supports a more sustainable and responsible manufacturing process, contributing to a greener future.

2. Interface: Interface, a global leader in modular carpet manufacturing, has implemented sustainability initiatives to reduce waste and energy consumption. Their Mission Zero campaign aimed to eliminate any negative environmental impact by 2020, focusing on innovative practices and sustainable materials. By prioritizing eco-friendly manufacturing, Interface has significantly contributed to reducing its environmental footprint and promoting sustainability within the industry.

- **Sustainable Carpet Manufacturing:** Interface, a global leader in modular carpet manufacturing, has implemented various sustainability initiatives to reduce waste and energy consumption. By adopting innovative practices and using sustainable materials, Interface has significantly lowered its environmental impact. The company's commitment to eco-friendly manufacturing practices has made it a pioneer in the industry, promoting resource conservation and energy efficiency while maintaining high-quality product standards.
- **Mission Zero:** Interface's Mission Zero initiative aimed to eliminate any negative environmental impact by 2020. Through this ambitious program, Interface focused on reducing waste, lowering energy consumption, and using sustainable materials in its manufacturing processes. By setting clear sustainability goals and implementing innovative practices, Interface significantly minimized its environmental footprint and set a benchmark for eco-friendly manufacturing in the industry. The Mission Zero initiative underscores Interface's commitment to creating a more sustainable and responsible future.

3. Unilever: Unilever focuses on sustainable sourcing, ensuring that raw materials are procured with minimal environmental impact. The company has also established green factories that use renewable energy and practice water conservation. These efforts reflect Unilever's commitment to reducing its environmental footprint, promoting resource efficiency, and supporting sustainable development. By implementing these eco-friendly practices, Unilever demonstrates its dedication to a greener and more sustainable future.

- **Sustainable Sourcing:** Unilever prioritizes sustainable sourcing by obtaining raw materials in ways that ensure minimal environmental impact. The company adheres to environmentally responsible practices, such as using renewable resources, supporting fair trade, and promoting biodiversity conservation. By prioritizing sustainable sourcing, Unilever aims to protect ecosystems, reduce deforestation, and support local communities. This commitment to sustainable practices helps minimize the environmental footprint of its products and contributes to the overall goal of creating a more sustainable and responsible supply chain.

- **Green Factories:** Unilever has established green factories that prioritize sustainability by using renewable energy and practicing water conservation. These factories are designed to minimize environmental impact by incorporating energy-efficient technologies and systems to reduce water consumption. By focusing on renewable energy sources and efficient water use, Unilever's green factories contribute to reducing greenhouse gas emissions, conserving natural resources, and promoting sustainable manufacturing practices. This commitment to eco-friendly operations supports Unilever's broader goals of environmental responsibility and sustainable development.

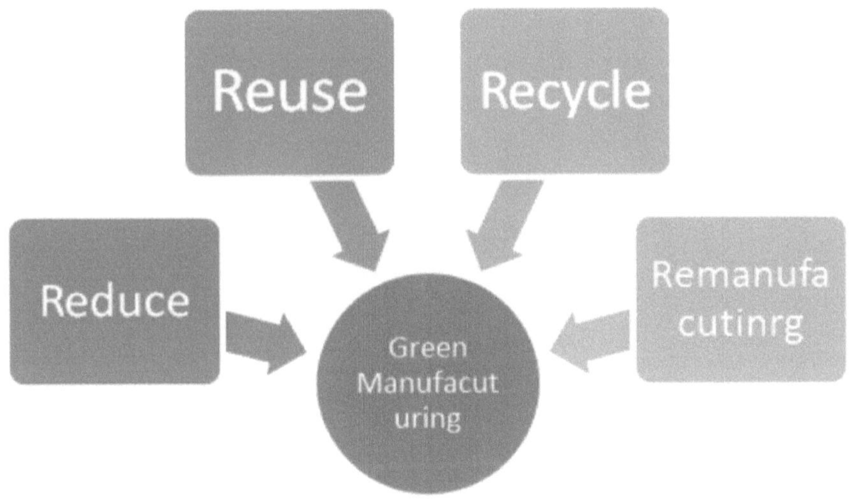

Green Manufacturing

Conclusion:

Sustainability and green manufacturing are crucial for shaping a more sustainable future. By embracing eco-friendly practices, businesses can lower their ecological footprint, cut costs, and cater to the rising demand for sustainable products. These efforts not only benefit the environment but also drive economic growth and enhance social well-being, creating a comprehensive positive impact on society and the planet.

www.ingramcontent.com/pod-product-compliance
Ingram Content Group UK Ltd.
Pitfield, Milton Keynes, MK11 3LW, UK
UKHW041637190726
13854UKWH00006B/2554

9 798899 067853